Dragonfly Notes:
ON DISTANCE AND LOSS

Anne Panning

stillhouse
press
CRAFT PUBLISHING FOR ARDENT SPIRITS
FAIRFAX, VIRGINIA

All inquiries may be directed to:
    Stillhouse Press
    4400 University Drive, 3E4
    Fairfax, VA 22030
    www.stillhousepress.org

Stillhouse Press is an independent, student and alumni-run nonprofit press based out of Northern Viginia and established in collaboration with the Fall for the Book festival.

LIBRARY OF CONGRESS CONTROL NUMBER: 2018937961
ISBN-13: 978-0-9969816-9-9

Designed and composed by Douglas Luman.

For
Mom
and
Lily

"Who would deduce the dragonfly from the larva, the iris from the bud, the lawyer from the student? ...We are all shape-shifters and magical reinventors. Life is really a plural noun, a caravan of selves."

Diane Ackerman

"Now I am setting out into the unknown. It will take me a long while to work through the grief. There are no shortcuts; it has to be gone through"

Madeleine L'Engle

Signs

My mother appears regularly to me in the form of a dragonfly—or so I like to think. I know this probably sounds like wishful thinking, or like some New Age talisman to ease the pain of grief. The fact is, I'm not sure. Go into any gift shop and you'll find a whole array of dragonfly paraphernalia: coasters, key chains, picture frames, magnets—even solar-powered dragonfly lights. Even before my mother died, I had a beautiful dragonfly trivet hanging in my kitchen and owned a pair of dragonfly earrings. There's something about them—what is it? Their gauzy gossamer wings, their prismatic rainbow coloring, their delicate, slender grace. There's a sacredness to them, a fleeting beauty I've since learned has come to represent transformation and life's ever-constant process of change. Some cultures, I've read, believe dragonflies to be the souls of the dead.

The other day, both of my children, Hudson and Lily, came rushing inside from the backyard. "There's a bug on the door handle!" Lily screamed. When I went to investigate, I saw a perfectly still dragonfly poised on the screen door handle. And I'll admit, I thought: Mom.

My husband, Mark, came to look with me. "I think it's molted and left its shell," he said. "I think it's dead." We all gathered around it. But when I touched it, it quickly flew away. My children know the dragonfly link I have to my mother, and though they're too young to truly grasp the loss I feel, they often point out dragonflies to me when we're out and about, kayaking on Hemlock Lake or waiting for the school bus in our front yard. "There's your mom," Lily will say proudly when she spots one, without a trace of sadness (she was barely three years old when my mother died). But every time she does this I'll catch Hudson looking at me sidelong, gauging my reaction, checking for tears. For so long I tried to hide my sadness from my children, not wanting to worry them, until my therapist noted that by doing so, they might come to believe it's best to hide all negative feelings and they might then learn to suffer worse when their own disappointments and sorrows come.

But here's the thing: I know that no dragonfly pillow or necklace or lawn ornament will ever take away the pain of my loss. Sometimes the grief still feels so fresh and raw that I'll stand under the warm water of my morning shower and cry until my head pounds. Grief is so private that it's hard to take it out into the world. At night in bed when I can't sleep, I'll lie there and play a game. "Okay, Mom, if you're really here, give me a sign. Anything. A flash of light. A car driving past, right at this very second."

But nothing happens.

A couple things did happen, though, immediately after my mother's death that gave me pause. After I returned from my mother's funeral in Minnesota, I flew back to New York, exhausted. A few days later, I walked very slowly up to my office at the university where I teach. I hadn't been up there in a long time, and classes would be starting back up soon. I didn't care. After witnessing death up close, I found it hard to care about teaching proper grammar or different fictional points of view.

It was a hot August afternoon and I felt utterly alone. The greasy tang of Buffalo wings hung in the air, as well as the perfumey smell of peoples' dryer sheets pumping out of vents. The sun shone down at a harsh angle and made maple trees, porch railings, and lawn chairs look surreal and hyper-detailed.

When the students were gone for the summer, Brockport had an eerie, silent quality that seemed to amplify its sadness. I walked down Holley Street—not my usual route, but since my mother's death, I'd begun changing everything about my life: grow out my short bangs, take a Pilates class, adopt new and unusual routes to familiar destinations. Holley Street was one of my new routes, lined with rambling, ornate Victorian houses turned student apartment rentals. It was a beautiful tree-lined street, but the houses had grown shabby and run-down. Plywood beer pong tables still adorned porches and beat-up bicycles were chained to each other like packs of wild dogs.

I was peering up at a stained glass window that had been smashed in when I stumbled over something. There, right in front of me, in the middle of the sidewalk, was a book: *Better Homes and Gardens Sewing Book: Custom Sewing Made Easy*. I picked it up; it was a hardback how-to manual with a retro 1950s look. On the cover was a red tomato pincushion, scissors, spools of thread, a tape measure, and a thimble—all the things I've always associated with my mother, an expert seamstress and quilter who could and did make everything, including my wedding dress. I clutched the book to my chest and brought it home.

My mind raced. Why would there be a book in the middle of the sidewalk? And what were the odds it was a sewing book? Sewing was not just a hobby for my mother; it was in her DNA, just like brown eyes and blonde hair. My mother had always wanted to teach me to sew. We had often talked about it, then laughed, since I could barely sew on a button. Someday, I always thought, I'll have her teach me. Someday when I'm not so busy. When the kids are older. When I go out to see her for a good long visit.

The single most iconic image I hold of my mother is her sitting in front of her Singer sewing machine at the dining room table, pins held between her teeth, measuring tape hung around her neck, yards of fabric spilling onto her lap. This was where she was most at home, most herself.

Later, I relayed the sewing book incident to my family back in Minnesota via a series of phone calls. My father, so broken and incapable of almost everything after my mother died, could only cry, sniffle, and moan.

My two brothers, Jim and Mike—construction workers, hunters, great lovers of the outdoors—didn't have much to say. Mike, younger than me by twelve years, had always accused me of looking for "drama" when there wasn't any, and he responded in kind. Jim, the oldest, quietest, and least willing to talk about anything emotional, said, "I mean, I guess you could think it was a message from her."

Then there was my little sister, Amy, my heart. She was the blonde to my brunette, the navy blue to my black, the uncluttered new-build to my cluttered old Victorian. Younger than me by three years, she lived about forty minutes from our parents' house, had married her high school sweetheart, and had three beautiful kids I adored. Because my job had taken me to New York (in my line of work, you go where the job is), she and I mostly caught up by phone while we both ran errands and rushed here and there with our kids. When I told her the sewing-book story, there was a long silence, until she finally said, "Anne, oh my God! The same kind of thing keeps happening to me." Despite our differences, we both agreed that it was absolutely a message from our mother: I still see you. I'm here.

About a month later, I was in Target shopping for some yoga pants and laundry baskets. As usual, I had to stop in the bathroom before I grabbed a cart. Inside the stall, lying on the toilet paper dispenser, was a small laminated prayer card—a pink oval with pressed ridges all around it. I picked it up, and read: *As a mother comforts her child, so I will comfort you—Isaiah 66.* I lost my breath for a second, and then a great warmth washed over my body as if I had walked into a tropical rain forest.

I pocketed the card, ended up losing myself in the bright, beautiful world of Target, and forgot all about it until later that night when I removed it from my back pocket, warm and molded to shape of my body. This time, I didn't tell anyone, not even Mark. It was a quiet, private message, I decided. It was a whisper from my mother. *It's okay. Be calm. I'm here.*

Yet another month later, I was driving between the three points of my daily triangle—day care, grocery store, campus—when I turned on the radio. I don't typically listen to the radio while driving, preferring my favorite CDs: Amy Winehouse, John Prine, Frank Sinatra, Lucinda Williams. This time, though, I scanned several stations before coming upon a loud gospel preacher. "And Jesus said, 'You are *not* alone! You! Are! Not! Alone!' This is what I'm saying to you, people, when you feel sad and lost. This is what I'm saying to *you*! You are *not* alone." I gripped the steering wheel before turning off the radio. Another message, I thought, from my mother? A peace settled around me as I drove home, made pasta primavera for dinner, put the kids to bed after reading to them from the original *Pinocchio*. But for the rest of the night, my footsteps felt airy. My fingertips seemed to touch everything with care and delicacy. When my head hit the pillow that night, it felt scooped in a cloud.

When I woke up, the feeling was gone.

Even though my mother came from a good middle-class family, sometimes I think she simply ended up in the wrong life. Despite her parents' protests—or perhaps because of them—she let herself be lured in by my father's daring bad-boy ways. I know that before my father, my mother had always been a good girl, and all of the photos I've seen of her support this: her prim Peter Pan collar blouses; her sweet, composed smile; the trusting way she gazed into the lens of the camera. The daughter of an award-winning butter maker and a nurse, she was raised in a no-nonsense religious family in a small Midwestern town seemingly untouched by the crazy, tumultuous sixties and seventies. When I used to ask her what things were like in Arlington, Minnesota during the Vietnam War, she'd shrug and say, "We didn't really notice it much. I was working at Dad's creamery and we just didn't buy into all that anti-war stuff." In the photos I've seen of her from this period, she wore hand-knit cardigans with shiny buttons, side-zip pedal pushers that accentuated her trim waist and hips, and a short but feminine haircut that made her high cheekbones and big brown eyes even more pronounced. Her hair was honey blonde; her eyelashes were long; her posture was poised and almost regal.

Her parents, Henry and Lucille Griep, were strict German Lutheran disciplinarians with six children. "If we didn't eat every last thing on our plates, Dad would bang his fist down on the table so hard our glasses would rattle. I could feel it in my bones. If anyone defied him, he'd scream in their face until his neck veins bulged, then storm out of the room. He was like an army sergeant." By age fourteen, my mother was in charge of cooking the family meals, while "the boys," her three brothers, got to play sports and run free. "We girls had to do the laundry, clean the house top to bottom, everything. Meanwhile, the boys would be shooting baskets in the driveway," my mother told me on more than one occasion.

Was this why she was drawn to such a party boy as my father? Was he the perfect act of rebellion against her authoritarian parents and her strict upbringing? My father even dressed the part of a "Rebel Without a Cause" in his tight white T-shirt, rolled-up jeans, Buddy Holly glasses, and black slicked-back hair. He was tall and thin. He was handsome and athletic. At one point, professional baseball scouts came swarming, eyeing him for the big leagues, but, as the story goes, just as things were moving closer to a potentially lucrative offer, my father was caught drinking one weekend and kicked off his high school team. It became his great tale of "almost," his story of near fame and glory he'd tell over and over to anyone who'd listen.

Next to him, in pastel shirtwaist dresses and pale pink lipstick, my mother was such an innocent. But when I look very carefully at the photos, really study them hard, there's something else in her eyes, too: a little sense of sneakiness, of getting away with something, a sort of silent flip-off to her good-girl upbringing. I wonder what she would think of my writing this. "That's not true and you know it!" she'd say. "You're always looking for more of a story than there really was."

There are so many things I wish I could ask my mother, and part of what I mourn is the gaps in my history—and hers—that I will never fill now that she's gone.

Did you and Dad have sex before you were married? (I may have been too shy to ask that one; I'm not sure.) Where did you stay on your wedding night? Did you have a honeymoon? Where did you go? And how did you ever afford it? Why did you marry Dad if you already knew he was such a heavy drinker? (I'd tried that one several times, but wish I'd pushed harder.) Was there anyone else you wished you had married instead? Did you and Dad use birth control? What did you see in him? Did he make you laugh? Did you snuggle on the couch and watch TV together? Where did you go on your very first date? Do you remember what you wore? When he went to barber school, did you ever let him cut your hair? When did you feel him start to disappoint you? Did you ever want to take it all back, start over, find someone else? Why didn't you? What made you stay?

But like many women in my hometown, my mother was long-suffering and loyal. Divorce was something for weak and selfish people who couldn't see the greater good their sacrifice would offer. From everything I know about my mother, she would endure whatever hardship came her way, all in the name of keeping the family together.

I don't want to memorialize my mother as saintly or heroic, though. For every single pleasant memory I have of her—the sight of her big red station wagon waiting to pick me up after school during a blizzard, for example, or the gorgeous peach voile prom dress she made me with satin ribbons that tied at the shoulders—there are at least two or three unpleasant ones: "Do you kids piss me off on purpose or does it just come naturally?" spit out in a frustrated rage while my siblings and I beat on each other in the back seat of the car. "Dammit! I have five dollars to get through this week," said through clenched teeth while rolling the grocery cart through the store, "so don't be asking for a single thing, do you hear me?" Her crying at the back end of the trailer while my dad was out drinking (this one oft repeated).

It was push-pull living with her as a mother. She'd be kind and loving one minute, reading me a book while I sat on her lap or French braiding my hair before school, then the next minute I'd find her smashing dirty pots and pans in the sink while she cried and swore, hunched over the mess. "Your father thinks he can just go out and do whatever he wants," she'd say, sniffling, "while I have to sit here with you kids! Do you have any idea how hard this is? Do you?" She'd brace herself against the counter with both arms locked stiffly at the elbows, cry some more, then eventually wear herself out and collapse in a chair. Somehow I knew even then that she wasn't really complaining *about* us, only *to* us. The rants were for my father, of course, who was rarely there to hear them. When he did come wandering home after the bar closed, I'd hear my mother attempting a fight with him, but by then he was too drunk for any real sparks to fly. Some phrases did carry down the skinny trailer hallway and into the bedroom I shared with Amy: "...drinking all our grocery money up at the bar..." and "Don't you even care about your own children?" and "...nothing but a goddamn drunk..." She'd hit him; I could hear the smacks and slapping. Thank God he never hit her back.

The truth is, I don't hold any of it against her. Or rather, I understand now, as an adult, how desperately she must've been trying to hang on, how precarious every single day must've felt to her. But what I don't understand, to this day, is why such a smart young woman would make so many bad decisions. By everyone's accounts, my father was already an alcoholic in high school when she dated him; he was an even worse alcoholic when they got married, and although he eventually quit drinking, he was still an addict to the core and eventually took up another addiction. And another. And another. He could not have been an easy man to live with.

Because I lived far away from the cemetery where my mother's ashes were buried, I felt the need to buy a memorial marker to have at my home in upstate New York. One afternoon in August, just a month after my mother died, Mark and I loaded up the kids and went to Sarah's Garden Center on the outskirts of Brockport. Going to Sarah's had always filled me with a sense of optimism; our children had grown up strolling the outdoor aisles in search of the brightest geraniums for our flower boxes or pink azaleas for the cool, shady north side of the house. Each Christmas, we'd pick a Christmas tree there, then we'd go eat at Barber's Bar & Grill, where the kids played pinball and drank Shirley Temples and Mark and I ordered Buffalo wings and beer.

At Sarah's, Mark and the kids gave me a wide berth while I searched long and hard through concrete statues of angels, spooky-faced and stern. There was Buddha in large, medium, and small. There were painted frogs, bunnies, ladybugs, gnomes, and, yes, dragonflies. Nothing was right—too religious, too goofy, too dreary—and I began to question the point of it anyway.

In the distance, I saw Mark and the kids pulling around a wagonload of flowers; Mark waved. I waved back at him, shrugged my shoulders, wandered around some more and eventually met them back at the register.

"Are you okay?" Mark asked, and pulled me close. He was aging well, with silvery highlights at his temples that contrasted nicely with his dark brown eyes. He'd started working out daily and was a fit and healthy 6'4".

"No," I said. "But yeah. You know."

He nodded. The kids were sticking their fingers into a birdbath fountain, then splashing each other, then yelling at each other for splashing each other. Behind them, up on a shelf, I saw the perfect thing: a rooster. It was just the right mix of country charm with a bit of ironic whimsy—the rooster had a wry, skeptical look on its face. It was about a foot tall, made of gray stone with a matte white wash that accentuated its feathers. Mark got it down for me; it weighed a ton.

"Is that for your mom?" Lily asked. She turned to look up into my face.

I said yes.

"So, like a gravestone?" Hudson asked. Sadly, the kids had not attended my mother's funeral, and as a result, my mother's death remained less real to them, almost fictional. My children experienced, instead, the post-apocalypse of death: the silent, stunned nature of grief instead of the open outpouring of emotion they would've seen at her funeral.

Back home, I obsessed over where to put the rooster. I wanted to see it from the kitchen window when I was washing dishes or cooking, but I also wanted it somewhere semi-private and cozy. After wheeling the poor rooster all over the backyard in the wheelbarrow, I finally settled on a corner of Hudson's little flower garden that he was kind enough to offer me. There, it would get southern sun almost all day, and would stand out in contrast to the dark dirt without being showy. Hudson's flowers would bloom around it, and the idea of that made me happy.

Mother's Day was gorgeous and sunny, and we all luxuriated in the backyard—Mark building a new garden bed, the kids playing Frisbee, me reading on the chaise lounge. From where I sat, I had a perfect view of the rooster, which sat wedged into the corner of Hudson's garden. I wished I could say it always reminded me of my mother, but the fact is, sometimes I don't even notice it anymore, tucked behind the newly planted purple delphiniums and sunflowers. It has become everyday, like my grief.

One day after my mother died, someone gave me *Stokes Beginner's Guide to Dragonflies*. It's small, about the size of my hand, a colorful, shiny, well-organized guide for whatever you'd call the dragonfly equivalent of a birder—a dragonflier?

Mostly, I like looking at the pictures of their lithe vivid bodies, their gauzy transparent wings. I like their names: "Calico Pennant," "Prairie Bluet," "Powdered Dancer," "Smoky Rubyspot," "Flame Skimmer," "Comet Darner."

I see my mother in these words: calico fabric draped over her lap at the sewing machine while she made kitchen curtains; *A Prairie Home Companion* on the radio as she washed the dishes; darning socks on a wooden egg while she watched Martha Stewart make "effortlessly elegant" centerpieces out of floating orchids and tropical fruit.

My mother's health problems began in an innocent, random way. For years my mother had struggled with a weak bladder, and whenever we got together, she'd beg us not to make her laugh because she'd end up peeing in her pants. "You kids, stop!" she'd say, crossing her legs and bouncing up and down. "I'm serious. Stop!" Whenever she'd sneeze, she'd say, "Well, there I go spritzing again." Her mother, my Grandma Griep, had had the exact same problem, and whether it was childbirth that had weakened the muscles, or simply genetics, my mother could barely walk a few blocks before needing to find a bathroom. Amy and I already showed signs of the same problem. I knew every bathroom in every mall, store, park, running route, and restaurant. We always joked that we all had bladders the size of a walnut.

Amy had started working as support staff at a local hospital, and as a result, she'd become familiar with the various doctors and nurses, and with the procedures there. It was at the hospital that she'd heard about a fairly new and innovative solution to incontinence that involved inserting a mesh sling underneath the bladder to lift it back into its normal position. The mesh sling provided support, like a hammock, so the bladder wouldn't sag down and cause constant pressure to urinate. The procedure was called an IVS Tunneler TVT. I never figured out what IVS meant, but TVT, I learned, stood for tension-free vaginal tape, the piece of mesh used in the surgery.

Before my mother had the surgery, I'd read mostly positive reports online. IVS was supposed to be a highly effective yet minimally invasive procedure that posed very minor risk of complications. Later, however, after my mother's death, I found pages and pages of law-firm websites devoted exclusively to complications caused by defective mesh materials. According to one website, since doctors began using the mesh slings for incontinence in the late 1990s, the FDA had received over a thousand reports and complaints from patients. Many of the problems involved erosion, in which the mesh protruded into the organs and the skin split, resulting in pain and infection. In some cases, the mesh would completely detach from the bladder area and migrate into the vaginal walls or other organs.

Of course, none of us knew these things before my mother had the surgery; the FDA did not put out an official public warning until 2008, four years too late for my mother. Plus, many women had reported swift and successful results. Even the Mayo Clinic's website, at the time, suggested the procedure was less invasive and less complicated than other surgeries used to correct pelvic organ prolapse (POP), the condition that caused my mother's incontinence.

Although it may not have been medically urgent, my mother's incontinence had begun to dominate her life. According to Amy, my mother could no longer go to the grocery store because they didn't have a bathroom there and she couldn't last through a whole shopping trip before she felt the urge to go. Just like my Grandma Griep, my mother kept an industrial-sized box of Depends stuffed in the bathroom cabinet, and her purse was always puffy with an emergency supply. She'd have to go badly in the middle of the night and couldn't make it fast enough to the bathroom, so eventually she kept an ice-cream pail by the side of her bed (as she'd confessed to me with embarrassment). When I heard she'd finally made an appointment for the procedure, I was thrilled. Good for her, I thought. A positive, proactive move. I remember jotting the date of her appointment down on my calendar: June 10, 2004.

This was where things got fuzzy. At this same time, I was nine months pregnant with my second child. Though I felt great, I'd had various complications with the pregnancy every step of the way, including placenta previa early on, and later, an amniocentesis that revealed a genetic translocation in the fetus, which my doctor explained in the following manner: "It's like you have all the right books on the bookshelves, but some of them are shelved in the wrong place." After more testing, it was revealed that I also had the exact same genetic abnormality, and since I was okay, likely my baby would also be okay. Still, a cloud of worry hovered over the pregnancy after that, and we were plagued by fears of having a baby with any number of genetic diseases.

In addition to all of this, I was also busy chasing around our three-year-old son, grading stacks of final papers, and desperately trying to finish the novel I was writing before giving birth. It was an incredibly stressful and busy time, and as much as I loved my mother and worried about her, I was consumed with my own life.

As luck (or unluck) would have it, Lily was born four days early in what was called a precipitous birth—read: dangerously fast. One minute I was sitting at home on the couch eating an apple when I felt a tiny ping inside me, and less than an hour later I was holding my daughter in my arms in a hospital thirty minutes away. In all the photos, my hair isn't even messed up; my eyeglasses are still on, and I'm wearing the same red T-shirt I'd been wearing on the couch. There was no doctor in the room, no time to get me off the gurney, and no time for my mind or body to process what was happening.

But the drama didn't stop there. Later that night, when we were still debating what to name her (Lucy? Lily? Vivian?), one of the nurses noticed she was spitting up green. "That's probably from the bile duct," she said. Mark and I looked at each other, concerned. "That can indicate problems in the digestive tract," the nurse said. "It's something we need to get checked out right away. But don't worry."

Don't worry? Of course we were worried, especially when Lily was whisked to the neonatal intensive care unit and no one came to report anything to us for what seemed like hours. Mark eventually had to go home and take care of Hudson for the night, while I was left with painfully engorged breasts and no baby to feed.

Later that night, I was led down to the NICU, but I wasn't allowed to see my daughter yet, as she was still being tested. A stern, pink-faced pediatric surgeon explained to me in a perfunctory manner that he wasn't sure yet what was wrong. As he scrubbed in at a deep metal sink, he said, "It could be any number of things. Worst-case scenario, cystic fibrosis. Or it could be a twisted or malformed intestine, which would require immediate surgery. Could be as simple as a meconium plug. Don't know yet." He glanced at me over the tops of his eyeglasses.

I crossed my arms over my chest. My breasts leaked milk all over my stomach, and milk dribbled onto my thighs. "Well, is she going to be okay?" I asked feebly.

He backed away from the metal sink, hands in the air. "Well, let's say this. I don't think she's going to die." That was the last I heard from him. I was sent back to the maternity ward, where I sat on the edge of my bed in the dim light waiting for someone to deliver the breast pump I'd been promised hours ago.

It turned out, thankfully, to be a meconium plug—the best-case scenario—but Lily still had to stay in the NICU until she passed regular stool, which ended up taking four nights. By the time we got home, I had no idea what day or time it was. I do remember a quick phone call to my mother. "Her name is Lily!" I said, to which my mother replied, "That's so beautiful it makes me want to cry!" which, of course, she did. I don't remember much beyond that. All I wanted was sleep and normalcy, neither of which was on the menu for the mother of a newborn.

The day of my mother's bladder surgery came and went, but I don't remember being aware of it. Only later, after talking to my sister and reading through my mother's medical records, did I realize how much blood she'd lost during that surgery, how she'd spent six days in the ICU with blood pressure so low she required almost constant transfusions, how close to death she'd come. There I was with a newborn fresh out of the NICU and there was my mother, a thousand miles away, in hypovolemic shock after what should've been a same-day surgery. Amy told me later that our mother had lost so much blood, she'd looked gray, almost corpse-like.

According to her medical files, my mother's bladder sling procedure on June 10, 2004 was "without complications and essentially no blood loss." However, later that afternoon, she had a hypotensive episode, and the doctor was called in immediately. He noted, "She was complaining of increasing left lower quadrant pain." An emergency ultrasound revealed "an acute pelvic hematoma that measured 14 x 8 cm." She was rushed to the ICU for multiple blood transfusions after her blood pressure dropped dangerously. After six frightening days of constant vigilance, she was sent home after being declared stable. Nothing, however, was further from the truth. She never felt good after that, she said. She was always in pain. She had almost constant bleeding.

At the same time, back in New York, Lily changed from a sleepy, happy newborn to an inconsolable, fussy baby. She slept little, nursed often, and at night turned into a crying little banshee who sucked the life right out of me. Mark and I both spent hours walking her through the house while she cried nonstop. During this time, we hosted much-anticipated family visitors—I wanted everyone to see our beautiful new baby girl! Mark's brother, Steve, and his family came to visit with their two kids three weeks after her birth; my sister, Amy, and her family came a couple weeks later, at my urging. The next month, Mark's parents came for a week. These were all invited and very welcomed family visitors, except that Lily had become such a difficult baby that I could barely function. It was almost impossible to carry on a conversation or sit down to a meal with Lily's constant wailing, much less entertain or enjoy our guests.

Of course, the person I really needed the most was my mother. I badly wanted her to see her beautiful new granddaughter. I wanted my mother's simple attention and maybe a little bit of her help, too. I remember one phone call when I asked her for about the tenth time when she was planning on coming out. If she waited too long, I told her, airfares would go up. Mark and I would have to start teaching again and we wouldn't have any time to visit. Lily was already almost three months old. My mother was missing all the good stuff: Lily's first smile, her new little Kewpie-doll hairdo, her tiny little legs kicking around in the baby bath. I remember how quiet my mother's voice got then when she told me she just didn't feel good, that she was in too much pain. "Annie, I just can't do it right now," she said. But in my sleep-deprived, postpartum, hormone-crazed mind, I remember thinking: How can you not want to come and see your new baby granddaughter? How can you do this to me?

Why don't you care? My mother's surgery had been weeks ago, I reasoned, and I figured she was probably just overreacting.

These were not my finest moments. I wish I could take them back, replace myself with a more understanding, open-hearted daughter who saw the pain my mother was going through and offered nothing but love and support. But I was so hurt, refusing to let the issue go, that my mother did come to visit that August, God help her. And of course, only later did I realize how badly she must've wanted to see Lily, as well. There are six photographs to prove it—six, that's all—and when I study them, not only can I see how miserably hot my mother was in our un-air-conditioned house, her short hair dark with sweat, but I can also see how exhausted she looked, physically drained, as if she were just barely present.

In all of the photographs but one she's lying on the couch. I can't imagine how she must've felt, how much healing her body needed, how much pain she must've been in just holding Lily, much less trying to play rambunctiously with Hudson. One of the photographs is precious, though, and I've since framed it and hung it in Lily's room. In it, my mother's feeding Lily her first solid food, a tiny bowl of rice cereal that my mother's holding in her elegant hands. Lily's wearing a terry cloth bib with an embroidered turtle on it that my mother made, and she's clutching the bowl in my mother's hand as if she never wants to let go. My mother is completely bemused by this. I'm off to the side, smiling, taking it all in.

Exactly a year later, my mother's post-surgery complications grew so severe that she required another surgery to fix the damage from the first one. More of the mesh tape had eroded throughout her body, this time through her vaginal walls. She was in agony, bleeding, and, ironically, suffering from terrible incontinence—the reason she'd had the procedure in the first place. Before all of this began, she'd been hoping not to have to go to the bathroom so often, or, at the very least, not to wet her pants every time she walked, sneezed, or laughed.

Another year later, Lily turned two. Hudson started kindergarten, and it finally felt as if our family of four was grounded and growing. But for my mother, two whole years after her allegedly low-risk bladder sling procedure, there were more health complications, more doctor visits and repair procedures. Her medical files were voluminous, daunting, and painful to read. "A dangling piece of sling mesh was found rather close to the bladder. About 2 cm of mesh was trimmed as close to the vaginal mucosa as possible. When this was done, the remaining mesh retracted out of the site. This should effectively close the vaginal defect hopefully."

It was this last sentence (poorly constructed with its double adverbs) that made me begin to question if someone, somewhere along the way, had screwed up. After all, the "defect" noted in the files did not exist prior to her surgeries. Was it then created by incompetent doctors, defective materials, lax follow-up care, or some combination thereof?

I've studied her medical records repeatedly, religiously, over the years, searching for a clear answer that doesn't exist, but there's one part in particular that always stops me. "I do not personally believe," wrote one doctor, "that there is a strong possibility of eradicating her problem." I have pulled apart this sentence too many times to count. Why? Why did he not believe this? Why did it sound like he was giving up?

I had only to read on for my answer. "She has residual mesh in the system, and if this is removed, she may worsen. I have offered her a second opinion by an expert in female urology at the Mayo Clinic. She has thought about it and deferred at this time."

I have asked myself over and over why she did not take him up on that second opinion. It would've been at the Mayo Clinic, a morning's drive away in Rochester, one of the best hospitals in the country. But part of me knows why. My mother hated hassles—she had no patience for chaos or confusion or hullabaloo. Plus, considering all she'd been through, I couldn't blame her. She was sick, tired, frustrated, and probably couldn't bear the thought of starting all over again with a new doctor. Who could blame her?

Still, the notion of "what if" will always linger.

John Deere Dress

The other day, I was driving home from the gym when I saw two girls walking up the hill toward the Erie Canal. They were maybe eleven or twelve, and one of them wore a dress that looked clearly homemade. When I peered more closely, I noticed it was a green and yellow John Deere tractor print. Huh, I thought. I had nieces that age and could not imagine them wearing such a thing. Instead, they preferred cargo capris and camis and flip-flops. The girl in the John Deere dress wore long braids. Somehow, the fitted pinafore style of the dress and her braids brought to mind Dorothy from *The Wizard of Oz*.

Without warning, I began to sob uncontrollably. It was all I could do to point myself home and park the car. I sat clutching the steering wheel, almost hyperventilating. I didn't want to go inside; I didn't want to try to explain to Mark something I could barely explain to myself. Eventually, I pulled myself together and very gently went to lay on the couch. Mark wasn't home, nor were the kids. Our little cockapoo, Martha, jumped up and settled next to me. I watched the newly unfurled maple leaves flutter outside the window.

What was happening to me? Here it was, almost four years since my mother had died, and the grief could still hit me so randomly I had to pull off the road? But it was true. Seeing the girl's homemade John Deere dress made me realize that my daughter, Lily, would never get to wear a pair of my mother's famous homemade flannel pajamas. She had sewn them for me when I was a kid and had then sewn a pair every Christmas for all of her grandchildren. She chose whimsical flannel (flying pigs, twirling planets, candy and lollipops) and novelty buttons (hearts, moons, stars, smiley faces). Hudson had been lucky enough to get a few pairs, but what about Lily? How would she ever come to know how gifted and warm and talented and wonderful my mother was? I could try to tell her, show her photos, but she would never really understand or appreciate it as I needed her to. Not completely.

Triggers, I thought, or as one of my grief books called them, "grief-bursts." These were something I'd talked to my therapist about recently. "Triggers bring you closer to your feelings quite suddenly," my therapist had explained. "It's perfectly normal." Still, they always caught me off guard, and only later, after some time, did they make sense.

My mother had sewn almost all the clothes I'd worn as a child. She was very gifted in that way, but I'd also come to understand how little money they had and that she'd done it out of economic necessity, too. I still had some of my favorite clothes she'd made tucked away in the cedar chest: my brown gingham baby dress with the white embroidered pinafore; the quilted Raggedy Ann jumper with red heart pockets; the mod 1970s green jumpsuit with macramé belt. My mother could sew anything, and she put great pride in what we wore—though, of course, as soon as I became a rebellious, surly teenager, nothing she could make was good enough for me. I had to babysit constantly and work the soybean fields all summer to afford a coveted pair of Levi's or a pair of leather Nikes with a red swoosh.

As I waited for the kids' school bus to arrive that day, I realized that the John Deere girl's braids had been the other trigger. I remembered how in junior high I'd grown my hair out long and would often wake my mother up very early in the morning and ask her to French braid it before school.

My mother would burrow beneath layers of cotton sheets, velour blankets, and a star pattern quilt. "Need coffee first," she'd say, but I had a comb and cup of water in hand and stood waiting impatiently. She'd braid my hair so expertly it would last all day and into whatever I had going on at night. When she was done, she'd pat me on the butt, turn on the TV, tuck her legs up, and sit staring like a zombie with a mug of coffee in her hand.

I can still feel the thin plastic comb sliding a clean part down the back of my head, the firm tug of hair as my mother's fingers worked my thin silky hair into place, the definitive snap of the rubber bands as she'd secure the ends and send me on my way.

All You Can Eat

The first time I returned to my parents' house after my mother's death, I wandered from room to room, unable to bear the sight of her belongings. In the bathroom, a tube of her Maybelline lipstick still sat on the shelf. I opened it and put some on, feeling the shape of her mouth against mine. Her terry cloth bathrobe hung from a hook on the door, and I grabbed it, smelled it, closed my eyes, and put it on. It smelled just as I remembered her: Caress soap and the warm dusty-almond scent of her body. I could not stay long in the house. An old Victorian, almost every room was wallpapered in a tiny floral pattern. The small rooms were crammed with old furniture, and piles of my mother's magazines, knitting projects, and fabric scraps covered the floor. It smelled like the vanilla candles she loved. Instead, I scurried off to my sister Amy's house, just an hour away but another world entirely, with its beautiful granite countertops, its open floor plan, its clean, sharp angles and lines. A place where we could forget.

The reason I found myself in Arlington again, just three months after my mother had died, was to promote my collection of short stories, *Super America*, which had just been published. The local library had invited me to do a reading and signing at the community center, and all of my local relatives—dozens of them—planned to be there. My grief was still so new and fresh that I wasn't sure how I'd be able to perform in front of an audience. When we walked in, though, no one was there. A stack of metal folding chairs sat in the corner. My heart fell. But gradually the room began to fill. My third-grade teacher,

Mrs. Mueller, still elegant with swept-back gray hair and sparkling eyes. My high school speech coach, Mrs. Kreft, with her enormous brown eyes and long black hair spiraled into a crown atop her head. My high school girlfriends—Janet, Mary, Kim, Patty, Jan, Pam, Carla, Anne. And then the relatives—John and Kandi, Beth and the kids, Sara and Jerry, Tom and Franny— so many of them that my heart caught inside my throat and I couldn't speak. Even my Grandpa Pader was wheeled in from the nursing home a few blocks away. "Well, Annie Girl," he said. "I always knew you'd be something. Huh? Didn't I always tell you that, kid? Ya, ya." My college friend, Birgit, scootched in at the last minute from Minneapolis.

Punch and cookies were served, and soon a squawking microphone was turned on and adjusted. I swallowed hard and pulled out everything I'd learned as a theater major: deep breaths, center of focus, point of fix.

But just then my mother's two lifelong best friends, Laura and Barb, walked in. They felt as familiar to me as any relative did. My mother had cleaned houses in Minneapolis with Barb for years. Laura owned Kick's Bakery on Main Street, and I remember both of them sitting around our kitchen table, visiting with my mother over coffee. Barb had short feathered hair, gold-frame eyeglasses and a hearty laugh that made her whole body shake. Laura was quieter, more of a listener, with blue eyes and dark hair and a distinctive mole on her face. They both came up to me and rubbed my back. "Your mom would be so proud of you," Barb said.

"Oh, she sure would," Laura said. "Too bad she's not here to soak all this in." As a child, I'd swum in her in-ground pool, backed away nervously from her big dogs, sunk my teeth into the warm raised glazed donuts she baked every morning for the bakery.

"Oh, boy," Barb said. "She'd be bursting her buttons." She smelled like peach lotion and wore a familiar top-and-slacks combination.

I could barely croak out a response; plus, in less than a minute, I had to go up to the podium and face everyone. I left Barb and Laura when a woman from the library tapped the microphone. I noted that when she introduced me as the daughter of Lowell and Barbara Panning, almost everyone seemed to look down. My mother's name had been spoken, and now the huge hole of her absence hit them. I saw Amy dabbing a Kleenex to her eyes. My father hung his head.

My Grandpa Pader, though, looked straight at me from the front row. He'd watched his wife, my Grandma Myrtle, die a slow, painful death; he knew. One of my friends, Patty, had lost both of her parents in a horrible car accident; she knew. My Aunt Harriet and Uncle Bert had lost their son, my cousin Lance, in his early twenties; they knew. Not many, it seemed, were immune—a fact that saddened and bolstered me simultaneously.

I began. I dedicated the reading to my mother. I said how good it was to be back in my hometown again. "But bittersweet, of course," I said. Everyone, it seemed, looked worried that I would break down then, but to my surprise, I did not. I read from a short story about a couple who start up a restaurant specializing in frog legs. It was called "All-You-Can-Eat," and I realized, too late, that it contained swear words aplenty. I saw the row of little old church ladies twist their mouths in discomfort. I read on: "In July, Kenner claimed, the frogs were screwing like crazy and making tadpoles left and right. 'They'll be lazy and sluggish and tired after all that sex,' Kenner claimed. 'Should be easy targets.'"

Oh, dear.

My sister put her hand over her mouth, stifling laughter. My Grandpa Pader listened intently, blinking behind thick bifocals. I kept going, unable to predict when the dirty parts were going to pop up. *My mother would just die*, I thought. And then I thought, Oh. And then I said, "Thank you, everyone, for coming."

Afterward, we all went to my Uncle John and Aunt Kandi's house, a mile out of town—smack in the middle of cornfields and surrounded by the enormous farm machinery parked around the periphery like hulking dinosaurs. Although Kandi was closer in age to me than to my mother, they'd grown tight over the years since they spent so much time together quilting and sewing and visiting. At times I had to fight off jealousy, especially when I'd call my mother and hear Kandi's kids laughing and playing in the background. "Oh, Kandi's just here with the kids and we're all just sitting around having a good time," she'd say. Sometimes I felt kicked in the stomach with longing. Why wasn't *I* there having a good time with *my* kids?

Of course, I had no one to blame but myself. I was the one who'd bailed on my hometown as soon as I was able. I didn't look back—at first. But since I'd become a parent, the distance that stretched between New York and Minnesota grew harder to bear with each passing year. I fantasized about living close to my parents—the kids piling out of the car on a random Sunday afternoon, my mother appearing on the back porch in her blue sundress with a pitcher of Kool-Aid, the kids upending the laundry basket of ancient Playskool toys my mother kept on hand.

Even when I did go back, it never took long before I got swept into the swirling family chaos that always, no matter what, existed. *Oh my God! Not a single person from X's family came to W's birthday party! Did you hear Aunt P and Uncle D are getting a divorce? Can you believe Dad lost his job again? We really have got to get Y to deal with that tax mess.* Although it was always heartwrenching to leave, I'll admit that I also felt relief and clarity to be returning to my own less tumultuous life.

At John and Kandi's, three slow cookers burbled away: sloppy joes, calico beans, and beer-cheese soup. Kandi, a tall and slender distance runner, was an excellent cook, and as everyone crammed into her tiny, narrow kitchen, she called out, "Come and eat!" in a loud and energetic voice. There was a great sense of fun and togetherness that, for a while, covered my mother's absence. My crazy cousins! Their kids running all around! My cozy Aunt Beth! My sweet uncle in his madras plaid shirt and khaki pants! Who made this amazing dip with cream cheese and apples? Apples! Who'd have thought?

Cameras flashed; everyone was eating and talking at high volume. Although we were not a drinking family, a couple bottles of white wine were uncorked.

"So how's everything out in New York?"

"Famous author now, huh?"

"So what's your next book going to be about?"

Of course, I couldn't tell anyone I hadn't written a word since my mother died, that I could barely read a book, much less write one. My father stood oddly by my side as I fielded these questions. Since my mother's death three months ago, he'd been plunged into an entirely new existence where he had to actually pay bills and do laundry and vacuum and face the world as a half instead of a whole. My mother was the social glue of his world and drew people toward them with her warmth and natural love of socializing. Without her, my father's tendency to withdraw and isolate himself kicked in strong. Even before my mother's death, he could often be found in their bedroom watching the Twins on TV while the rest of us yucked it up out in the living room. During Christmas gatherings, you could count on him disappearing to Food 'N Fuel (he called it "Foody") to go buy a Coke and escape. He couldn't sit still, yet he never really accomplished or did anything. Since my mother's death, my siblings and I had encouraged him to join a bowling league or volunteer at the nursing home, but his ever-present lack of initiative continued to hold him back.

Later, someone proposed a toast, and said, "Speech! Speech!" to me. Suddenly the tone went from silly to sober. I found myself opening up the can of grief by saying how badly I wished my mother could've been there to see my book published and to celebrate with everyone like this. "It's just..." I found myself pausing. "It's not the same without her." My father put his arm around me. My siblings all seemed shell-shocked because, I realized, they were.

Others joined in with comments about her, and though it was incredibly sad, it was also nice, and I was grateful for it. Her funeral at the conservative Lutheran church had been a cold, stodgy affair with no personal touches. It had actually pissed me off that all the pastor could manage to say was what a "great lamb of God" my mother had been, how she'd been baptized, confirmed, married, in the church. We all welcomed, I think, the chance to remember her personally.

But all good things end. I needed to get back to New York and teach and continue my book tour. As we all said goodbye and people began to leave, I started to wonder how many more occasions there would be like this to get together with my mother's family. Later, as I boarded the plane, a new kind of worry crept up on me. Without my mother, would my place at these family gatherings naturally fade? Had I not only lost my mother, but also my link to cousins, aunts, and uncles?

One day I stop over at my friend Christine's house. She's recently remodeled her bathroom, and though I've seen some of the progress on Facebook, I'm eager for a personal tour. Lovely lavender walls, dark espresso cabinets, beautiful brushed nickel knobs and faucets. Also, because she's leaving for a two-week summer vacation, she's asked me to "babysit" their goldfish, Creamsicle. It's just a tiny thing in an old-fashioned bowl, but I know my kids will be thrilled. After she gives me all of the instructions, we talk about a friend of hers who recently lost a child, and the way butterflies have begun appearing to her as a symbol.

I nod knowingly. I tell her that for me, it's dragonflies. "Sometimes when I'm jogging along the canal, swarms of dragonflies will hover over me. Last time I went running, one particular dark blue one escorted me the whole way out and back."

"Really?" Christine says. She then relates that when she walks along the canal, she never sees them. "Isn't that odd?" she says.

Christine is no stranger to grief; she lost her father in her early twenties, and I know the grief can still sometimes bring her to her knees. "For me, it's egrets," she says. "They always remind me of my dad because he and I used to see them a lot. And for my mom, it's hummingbirds."

I tell Christine that I should probably get going, hug her and wish her safe travels, then very gingerly carry the fishbowl down the street to our house.

As I walk up to the back door, a dark blue dragonfly flits up in front of me, swoops down by my feet, then flies away.

Grief Dog

After my mother died, I began searching frantically for a dog. I scoured the want ads; I looked online; I asked dog walkers who went by my house where they'd gotten theirs. Despite Mark's reluctance and his gentle reminder that I didn't even *like* dogs, I was absolutely determined to get one as soon as possible. It was all I could think about. And poor Mark. What could he do? How do you reason with someone who's just lost her mother?

While my mother was in the ICU in Minneapolis for almost a month, we would occasionally go to Amy's house to regroup, gather supplies, and shower. There, I'd found great comfort in their dog, Maisie. She was a good-natured, cream-colored cockapoo, and I loved the way she wedged herself right up against me when I sat on the couch. Plus, there was something about the simplicity of interacting with an animal, the easy way she both accepted and provided pleasure that made me cling to her in the chaos of my mother's precarious health situation. Although I'd always been notoriously *not a pet person*, I became convinced after my mother died that having a little dog just like Maisie would help me heal.

It's hard to stress how much I've always disliked pets of any kind. When dogs would come and try to lick me, I would push them away brusquely. I couldn't get excited about someone's guinea pig or hamster or ferret. I threw my mom's cats off the couch if they got in my way. It was everything I could do to tolerate our friends' big drooly dog when we went over to their house for dinner. Thankfully, Mark and I were very much in agreement that we would never be pet people. "Don't you just hate those pet owners who let their dogs run loose? And then they say things like, 'Oh, Buddy wouldn't hurt a fly! He's a real sweet dog.'"

My Grandma Griep used to say there was something wrong with people who didn't like animals. "It's just not right," she'd say, rocking back and forth in her glider rocker and pointing a sneaker. "People who don't like animals are missing something inside." She'd pop a butterscotch disc in her mouth and click it around. "Everybody should love animals, Annie." She'd actually wag a finger at me.

Finally, we found an old-fashioned pet store in Rochester: Al's Pet Shop on Ridge Road. When we told the owner, Al—a tall, fat man with light fuzz covering his head—that we were looking for a cockapoo, he cut right to the chase. "Boy or girl?"

"I want a girl dog," I said. Mark shrugged: *fine.*

"Well, then this here," Al said, "is the girl." He led us over to a little Plexiglass pen full of squirming puppies. "She's the only she. Plus she's the runt of the litter. Probably be on the tiny side." He scratched at the puppies' pink bellies with fingers fat as cigars. "Her brothers keep crowding her out from the mama's nummies."

Al held her up. She was tiny and fuzzy and cute; with her apricot coat, her big brown eyes and her shiny black nose, she looked just like the Boyds Bears I used to have as a child. But she was skittery. When Al handed her over to me, I panicked. I could feel her frantic little heartbeat in my hands. She was all rib cage underneath the fuzz. I set her down and she peed. Mark met my eye as if to say, "Are we really doing this?"

I nodded.

My mother had always loved animals, especially cats. At the time of her death, she was down to just two: Murphy and Kiki, or, as I called them, Ratface and Rhino. (Despite my mother's scolding, I knew she secretly loved when I did this.) The cats always gravitated right to me when I came over. "Well, look at that," my mother would say. "They sure do know who loves them the best." I'd push them away with my foot. She kept their litter box in the front entryway of the house, and whenever I visited, the distinctive tang of cat pee hung in the air.

Every time I called her, we went through the same routine. "Hey, it's me," I'd say.

"Annie!" she'd say. We'd chat for a couple minutes, and then, inevitably, she'd interrupt with, "Just a minute. Kitty! *Kitty!* Get down!" I'd hear the phone clunk down and the sound of shuffling. "Get down, I said!" She'd pick the phone back up. "Sorry. Murphy's trying to eat the aloe plant. Anyway." Then we'd continue, and then there'd be more cat scolding, and so it went with every single phone call.

Growing up, our family had had a dog, too. Lowbar (a combination of my mother's and father's first names, Lowell and Barb) was a German Shorthaired Pointer, a hunting dog, kept outside in a kennel behind the garage. When Lowbar died of cancer at an advanced age, I'd never seen my family so distraught. Though I did feel a slight sadness, I was amazed by the depth of their grief.

And yet years later, here I am with Martha, my own little cockapoo. We've grown to love her, of course, although we're not the best about getting her out for walks or making sure she gets her heartworm pills precisely every thirty days. But we are very good at cuddling with her; we've taken her kayaking and camping; I sometimes buy her Pup-Peroni at the grocery store; we get her cute haircuts at The Dog Wash, even though the groomer always scolds us a bit for waiting so long and allowing terrible mats to develop.

Hudson, to my horror, lets Martha lick him all over his face. Lily talks to her in a really high-pitched baby voice and tries unsuccessfully to make her sit and stay. Mark is hot and cold with her. When she gets tangled between his legs while he's trying to empty the dishwasher, he'll shout, "Dammit, Martha! Get out of the way!" But then he'll rub her belly and say, "Oh, Martha. You're such a good dog. Aren't you, Martha? Huh? Yes, you are."

If my mother could see this, she would be shocked. I sometimes want to believe she can see it all. I imagine how she'd laugh so hard she'd slap her knee, exclaiming over and over again how there is just no way she can believe we actually have a dog. "You, Annie?" she'd say. "With a dog?" She'd look at me with that bemused sparkle in her dark brown eyes. "I never thought I'd see the day."

Then she'd go cuddle Martha in her lap, gather Lily and Hudson around her, and tell them how afraid I used to be of dogs. "Your mom was even shy with people," my mom would tell them. She'd ask if I wouldn't mind pouring her some Pepsi with ice and I'd say sure. "When we used to go places, your mom would cling to my leg and hide behind me because she was so scared of everything. Especially dogs." I'd hand her the glass of Pepsi with a straw and we'd all sit around in the back sunroom as the day unfolded.

She'd throw Martha her squeaky rubber steak and laugh when Martha couldn't find it, even though it was right in front of her. I can still hear that laugh—more like a chuckle, really, ending in sigh of pleasure. "Ah, that dog of yours, Annie," she'd say. "She's just the cutest, dumbest little dog, isn't she?"

Hijacked

After I graduated from college in 1988 with a degree in English, I decided to join the Peace Corps. At the time, I was one of those rare English majors who wasn't particularly interested in teaching; my options for the future, consequently, seemed limited. I knew two things: I loved to write and was fairly good at it, and I someday wanted to apply to MFA programs in fiction writing. But after working three jobs simultaneously to put myself through college, in addition to acting in plays, writing reviews for the campus newspaper, and managing a turbulent relationship with my wrestler/poet boyfriend, I really needed a break. I was also without any money and wanted to travel, so I dutifully filled out my application for the Peace Corps, checking Southeast Asia as my desired location.

My mother was understandably saddened by the news that I'd be leaving for the Philippines for two years just weeks after my college graduation. "But we never see you as it is!" she said, which was true and not true. I still came home to visit, though sporadically. My life had slid in a significantly different direction than theirs, and going home to Arlington no longer held the cozy comfort and familiarity that it used to.

To her credit, my mother never tried to talk me out of it, not directly, but she did employ her favorite tactic, one she'd learned well from her own mother, my Grandma Griep: the guilt trip. "Well, you know I'm going to be sick with worry the whole time you're gone," she said. "I won't have any way to contact you. And God only knows what'll happen if you get sick out there in the middle of nowhere. Oh my God! I don't know how I'm supposed to get through two whole years like this." (She was an expert at shifting the focus from me to her.)

Recently, in her belongings, I found the letter I'd given to her at the airport just before my departure.

July 4, 1988

Dear Mom,

<u>BE POSITIVE.</u>

For me, please, these next couple of years. I need you to be happy. More than anything in the world I want that.

I will miss you and your warm wonderful face. I really will. In the throes of jungle life I will miss you dearly.

Please write. I need you to. I love you for everything you do for me, for what you've taught me to be, for being able to see me off on this long trip.

Be positive!

I love you,

Annie

My mother dedicated a good chunk of her time to worrying— about money, about tornadoes, about one of us falling down our steep stairs and breaking our necks, about the bats that occasionally got into the house in summer, about my father losing a limb at the factory where he worked, about one of us kids falling off our bikes and getting a head injury. Some of it was typical parent worry, but most was pure neurotic obsession over "what if."

I had to admit, it was hard to leave. I was only twenty-two years old and had barely traveled anywhere, except to my grandparents' cabin a few hours away. And what did I know about teaching English anyway? I'd never really done it; not *really*. And what if I *did* get sick? What if I got hurt or lost or couldn't take it over there? What if I wanted to leave early? What if they didn't let me? What if—? I was becoming as good at worrying as my mother.

But unlike her, I did leave Minnesota—tears and all—and it would change the course of my life forever.

I met Mark as a fellow Peace Corps volunteer in the Philippines. Mark's story of our meeting is far more romantic than mine; I'd joined the Peace Corps partly as a way to be alone and take a break from any romantic entanglements. Of course, I met Mark immediately. He was a tall, thin, dark-haired smoker with smoldering eyes. From Washington state, he'd recently graduated with a psychology major from the University of Washington-Seattle, and was a self-proclaimed reggae lover. We were all posing, really, reinventing ourselves for a life abroad. I found myself playing up my love of Russian literature and my penchant for drinking dark beer (though I'd only ever had one Guinness in my life).

During one of the icebreaker sessions, I remember Mark saying his dad was a nuclear engineer, and his mom was a Catholic school secretary. Okay, I thought. He's from a good family, unlike me. When it was my turn, I said, "My dad's a..." I don't even remember what job my dad had at the time I was in the Peace Corps. He might've been unemployed or driving a bread truck or painting farmhouses or selling Amway. I didn't want to get into it and out myself as trailer trash. Instead, I said, "My dad used to be a barber." That's how he started out anyway.

Mark's story of our meeting, however, is filled with romance and drama. "I remember I was standing in a room full of Peace Corps volunteers," he would tell people on occasion, "and out of the corner of my eye, I saw this flash of dark red—Anne's dress. Before I even registered her as a person, my heart dropped to my stomach and I could hardly breathe. When I could finally focus, I saw this girl with long brown hair and glasses, wearing a dark red jumper with a navy blue T-shirt under it. I just knew immediately. It was love at first sight. I knew I had to be with her."

Each Peace Corps volunteer was assigned to a region, one through eight, with one being the farthest north and eight being the farthest south. I was placed in region three, and when I found out Mark was placed in region eight, the disappointment was palpable, though I tried to hide it. Still, I reminded myself why I'd joined the Peace Corps in the first place: to escape romantic entanglements with needy and difficult boyfriends. It would all be better in the long run.

My experiences in the Peace Corps were a true test of my endurance for isolation and solitude. It turned out that many rural Filipino schools agreed to take on Peace Corps volunteers, but once we got there, they didn't know what to do with us. During my first month in San Pablo, Pampanga, I sat like a mannequin on display in the dim little high school library while students and faculty came by to sneak peeks at me through the open slatted windows. I tried to offer any service I could think of—grading papers, leading discussion groups, subbing for teachers if they needed time off—but that wasn't the way things worked. They had everything covered and didn't seem to want to change a thing.

The principal, Mrs. Lintag, was brusque and bossy with me. "You will go to meet the mayor now," she'd say, then have some random guy zoom me over to his house on a motorcycle. "You will be the Miss USA for our United Nations Day parade," Mrs. Lintag said, then had some shy, giggly schoolgirls dress me up in a red, white, and blue striped Uncle Sam top hat and a silver Miss USA banner over my chest. But most days were extremely quiet and lonely. Some days my only interaction was with the woman who sold bloody-bloody soup in front of my house on the river. Because of the language barrier, we'd nod, slap each other on the arms, and laugh. Then, when that was over, I'd skulk back into my house and read for the rest of the day.

On occasion, Mark and I would get together in Manila with other Peace Corps volunteers and we'd really cut loose. One night we were dancing and drinking at the Firehouse Bar; I believe I was smoking a Hope cigarette and staring drunkenly, pensively, at the strippers. Mark was behind me, ordering another beer, and I motioned for him to come over.

"I wish you would just kiss me already," I said.

Mark took a long drag on his cigarette and scrunched up his eyes. "What?" I loved his long fingers, his eyes so dark brown they were almost black, the way his faded Levi's hung off his hipbones.

"Why don't you just do it?" I said.

After months of listening to me rant about my need to be alone, to avoid any romantic relationship, Mark was understandably confused. Actually, so was I. I was such a bad drunk.

He did kiss me—right in the middle of the loud, smoky bar while our Peace Corps friends looked on. Later, one of them would say, "I knew it was only a matter of time. We were all just wishing you guys would get it over with already." And so, without much fanfare, we became a couple, separated by the chain of 7,100 islands that make up the Philippines.

During this time of our dramatic international courtship, I was woefully out of touch with my family back home. At the time, email, Facebook, texting, and cell phones were all nonexistent.

Even telephone calls were extremely hard to come by. Instead, I would write my mother voluminously long letters on thin onionskin paper, detailing every little aspect of my days.

And then for lunch I walked to the sari-sari store and bought a cucumber. I washed it in iodine water, then peeled it and sliced it into circles. My favorite sauce is to mix banana ketchup with mayonnaise to dip the cucumbers into it. Sounds weird, but it's really good. Later, an old woman with no teeth knocked on my door and asked me in Kapampangan something I couldn't understand but after about ten minutes I realized was a request that I come to her house and meet her son. Everyone, it seems, wants me to marry their sons and take them to America. So, how are you?

I didn't mention Mark in my letters to her at first; I'm not sure why.

The whole two years I was in the Peace Corps, my mother was a terrible correspondent, and even on the rare occasion when she did write me a letter, hearing from her always brought me down because it made me realize how much I missed her. It was the classic "ignorance is bliss" phenomenon: if I didn't hear from her, I could simply float along in my own little protected world and not notice how homesick I was. Her news, too, was always bad: Dad lost his job; my little brother got kicked out of school; Dad messed up his knee playing softball and couldn't go look for another job; they'd lost their health insurance due to my dad's unemployment. Over time, I realized the news was never about her but always about everyone else's problems, which she had to manage. My role as her daughter had morphed over the years into her confidante/cheerleader/therapist.

"Do you think I should leave your dad?" I remember her asking me while we'd walked the streets of Arlington one dark night. "I just can't take it anymore! But what would I do? How would we get by?" I'd been thirteen years old at the time, and felt my allegiances split cleanly in half like the separation of an atom: Mom versus Dad. Every time I read in one of her letters about all of the stress she was carrying, a nugget of guilt lodged deeper inside me: I'd abandoned her. Again. How would she cope?

As time progressed, I told her, little by little, about Mark. *So I met this guy named Mark. He's from Seattle and he's this cute, tall, skinny guy with dark hair and dark eyes and I think you'd really love him! He's really smart and funny and we're just friends because I told him I just didn't want to be in a relationship right now. He's so cute...*

I didn't know what the future held, and was trying very hard not to worry about it, but that was all thwarted when, out of the blue, a Peace Corps volunteer was kidnapped by members of the communist insurgency, and we had to be evacuated immediately. Finding ourselves suddenly in Manila, and then in Hawaii, Mark and I had to face the future much sooner than we'd thought. What to do? The best we could come up with was for him to go back to Washington and me to Minnesota, where my sister was due to have a baby any day. Mark would come out for a visit, and then we'd see. The famous Nietzsche quote came to mind: "We create ourselves by our choices," which was exactly what happened: Mark moved to Minnesota shortly after our Peace Corps evacuation in 1990, and by the fall of 1991 we were engaged.

The first time I brought Mark home to meet my family, I was nervous. I worried that once he saw how loud, chaotic, and dysfunctional we all were, how shabby our house was, how certain family members loved talking about farts and bowel movements and other happenings in their digestive tracts, he'd surely have to reconsider. It's not that his family was fancy in any way, but they were good, wholesome Catholics with a nice split-level house. They played hearts and cribbage for fun, tended to their lawn regularly with timed sprinklers, and went on hearty, interesting camping trips in their tent trailer. They were no-nonsense, stalwart people who would, I guessed, cringe with embarrassment and discomfort if someone farted in the room and then began describing the smell. In short, they were the kind of family I'd always dreamed of having.

I remember thinking that bringing Mark home to my family was like inviting a foreigner into a different culture. Mark was a newspaper and CNN junkie; strong-willed and opinionated, he loved a good argument—the more complicated, the better. My family, on the other hand, tried to avoid conflict at any cost, and didn't concern themselves much with politics or current events. And there was something else: Mark answered questions honestly when they were asked, stated his preferences and opinions. This was neither a good thing nor a bad thing, but strange to all of us who'd been raised in a milky haze of indecision, chaos, and passivity.

If my mother was over at someone's house for dinner and they asked her what she'd like to drink, she'd say, "Oh, whatever you have is fine." Then, when they'd list the options—beer, wine, Sprite, Coke, milk—she'd wave her hand and say, "Whatever you're having." Then, when the host would say it was up to her, my mother would say, "I don't know. Coke, I guess. But only if you have it. Milk is fine, too."

But most of my fears and insecurities turned out to be unfounded. Mark hit it off well with my family, especially with my brothers and my father. "I don't know what you were so worried about," Mark said to me later. "They're tons of fun. They're hilarious. I love them."

Something about my mother's reaction to Mark, though, seemed off, but I couldn't put my finger on it exactly. She was pleasant enough to him and never made any negative remarks, but I could feel her holding back. And sure enough, when I called her almost a whole year later from Bowling Green, Ohio, where Mark and I were getting our masters' degrees and planning our wedding, my mother finally came out with it.

"Well, I don't know how to say this," she stammered, "but I guess—well, I want you to really reconsider this marriage."

I froze on the other end. "What?" My heart thudded in my chest. "What are you talking about?"

"Well, now don't get so upset," she said. I could hear the turn in her voice. This was something she'd clearly been building up to, and I didn't like the sound of it. "I just think that Mark tries to control you too much. I think he tries to tell you what to do, and I'd hate to see you get involved in something you can't get out of... I mean, it's not like he abuses you or anything, but he seems to sort of dictate how things go in an abusive way..." Again, she trailed off.

I was completely dumbfounded. *Mark? Abusive?* The ironic thing was that Mark was the one boyfriend I'd had who was normal and functional. In fact, our relationship was so healthy it sometimes worried me. I'd had an abusive relationship before; my college boyfriend, Jonathan, had thrown a book bag at me and tried to choke me. *That* was abusive.

"What the fuck?" I asked. "Where is this *coming* from?" I hadn't spoken to my mother with this much venom since I was a sophomore in high school and she'd tried to ground me for spending a whole night out without telling her where I was. I had most certainly never sworn at her before.

My heart raced. I knew I was stronger than her, or at least more forceful. I could feel her backing down and becoming passive-aggressive. "Well, I never should have said anything," she said. "Now you're all mad at me."

Again, it was amazing how she could do this—turn it around to being her problem, my fault. I tried to be calm; I paced around our apartment, closing the curtains for no reason. "Just tell me what you're really saying. Tell me exactly what makes you say this."

She then went on to tell me what she'd witnessed the previous Thanksgiving, when I'd brought Mark to dinner at their house. I thought it had all gone reasonably well, save for my father rushing to the bathroom, moaning and groaning in the middle of the meal. Save for the fact that my dad loved to talk about bodily functions, no matter what the occasion. Save for the fact that my father actually returned from the bathroom chronicling the "movement" he'd just had. "Well," my mother continued, "he actually told you that you had to eat everything on your plate," she said. "As if you were a child."

My mind spun; I had absolutely no recollection of it.

"Then he said that if you didn't clean your plate," she went on, "you'd be in big trouble."

She waited, but I said nothing. I honestly could not get my mind around what she was saying.

"Annie, sometimes it's hard to see it when you're right in the middle of it," she said, her voice softening. "But I'm your mom. I have to watch out for you. I just don't like the way Mark talks to you."

After a minute, I vaguely remembered the conversation. We'd been kidding, of course, sarcastically ribbing each other, as was our way. I remembered us laughing. We'd been teasing each other, and it had gone both ways. I remember trying to force him to eat green beans because I knew he hated green beans. I'd even put a puddle of them, served in cream and butter sauce, on his plate. My mother didn't seem to remember that part.

"Will you just consider it? Will you think about this?" my mother said. "I just want you to be happy. I want you to be in a good relationship."

Then, as if someone had pulled the cork out of a bottle of champagne, I exploded. "You wouldn't know a good relationship if it hit you in the face!" I said. "You and Dad have pretty much *the* shittiest marriage I've ever witnessed in my life, and now *you're* trying to dole out marriage advice to *me*?" My parents had never seemed happy together. In fact, the majority of my recollections of them as a couple involve my mother in tears, my father drunk and trying to apologize. Over the years, they barely spent any time together at all. It was always Dad at the bar or out playing softball every weekend and Mom at home with us or, more often than not, at her parents' house where she could be cared for and treated like she was still a child.

"Why would you do this?" I asked, deflating. "Right before my wedding!" Thankfully Mark had gone out for a run and wasn't around to hear any of this. "Why would you go and say something like this and ruin everything just when things are supposed to be happy and good for me?"

Suddenly, though, it made sense: her wistful comments whenever I'd tell her how much fun Mark and I had camping one weekend, or how we'd made homemade pizza out of three random ingredients, or how we'd often get in the car, go driving, and not stop until something looked interesting. "I wish your dad was more like that," she'd say. "All he wants to do is lay around and sleep. Or go sneak off to the casino and blow his whole paycheck."

Now I started to see where this was coming from. Before Mark, all my other boyfriends had always been questionable: one was a motorcycle-driving meth addict who refused to wear underwear; one thought he was Billy Idol and became so obsessed with me that I had to get a restraining order against him; one was so jealous when I talked to other guys that he'd beat his knuckles against the dashboard of his car until they bled; one had dropped so much acid that his face twitched.

It's not that I believed my mother ever wished for my unhappiness—not at all. But I sometimes wonder if my dysfunctional relationships with men kept us somehow on equal footing. Sure, I'd managed to get myself into college, pay my own way, write and publish books, go and live all the way across the world by myself, but my proclivity for loser boyfriends was something we both shared. By marrying someone like Mark who was actually "normal" and functional and not an addict or unemployed or otherwise fucked up, would I be breaking our last bond, one we'd always shared? Was I bailing on her and leaving her to drown in her own unhappy marriage? Or, on a more positive note, did she want to protect me from marriage, given what she'd been through? I was still pretty young at the time, and maybe she thought I'd be better off waiting. I don't remember thinking rationally about it at the time. All I could see was my own mother trying to hijack my wedding.

"I think you're jealous," I said. "You're jealous because I have a good relationship with Mark, something you'll never have. I can't believe this." I practically snorted in disgust. "I have to go now. Bye."

I slammed the phone down. I was shaking so hard that I had to hold onto the kitchen counter for support. For the rest of the afternoon, I lay in our tiny bedroom, staring out of the window at fresh new maple leaves fluttering in the wind. Yes, Mark was assertive and not wishy-washy Midwestern like everyone my mother knew, but he was also kind, funny, reliable, and in no way, whatsoever, abusive . . . unlike my father, whose alcoholism, emotional inaccessibility, and lack of financial responsibility for his wife and children could definitely be construed as such. How could my mother be so blind?

But because we were a family completely terrified of conflict, neither of us knew how to resolve the issue. I wish I could say we had a nice, long heart-to-heart talk that patched things up, but that's not how I remember it. Like most things in our family, it was swept under the rug until another trauma reared its ugly head, which it always did.

In the aftermath of our fight, not to mention during the wedding itself, my mother and I never circled back to her concerns about Mark. Besides, it was a done deal; I'd moved on and away. Mark and I returned to Ohio, and, with the safety of distance protecting me, began our married life together.

As time went on, I'd occasionally remember the cruel words my mother and I had exchanged that summer, but the sting of it left me. Over the years, she grew to love Mark and accepted him fully into our family. She'd tease him about his West Coast accent, and he'd tease her about her Minnesota one. She grew to see what a good person he was, and more importantly, how much the two of us loved each other. Still, there was always a little edge between them, just a bit.

Post-it Apologies

Recently I came across a small collection of notes my father wrote to my mother. They were scribbled on all sorts of torn envelopes, paper, and Post-Its—red, teal, pink, yellow, green. Leave it to my mother to save absolutely everything—a trait I'd inherited, as evidenced by the stash in our attic of old newspapers ("Obama Is President!"), antiquated technologies (rotary phones, Brownie cameras), and even a stash of my old Levi's that I kept thinking the kids might want to give to their grandkids someday.

I laid all the notes out on my desk to form a colorful block quilt pattern. Most were tiny, extremely short and fragmented. *Very talented, Very beautiful. I love you, Me.*

How sweet, I thought. Such a contrast to the horrible way I remembered him treating her: blowing all his paycheck at the bar, leaving her to deal with four kids on her own, coming home drunk. There were other notes, equally pleasant, and if a person hadn't known the true history of their relationship, they'd surely think these notes were written by the most loving and affectionate husband ever.

You are so very beautiful. Love you.

Or, *I am one lucky man to have you as my wife. Love, Me.*

Or, *My Hon, you are beautiful, you are talented, you are a good mother, you are a good wife, you are mine and I love you. Love, Me.*

Sometimes I worried that I didn't give my father enough credit, that perhaps he wasn't as bad as I thought. But then I kept reading the notes, especially a longer one written on a company memo pad back when he was a Tastee Bread deliveryman. The letter was really more like a single-stanza poem, written in all capital letters in his distinctive feathery handwriting. It wasn't dated. It was wrinkled, shredded along the edges, and stained with food and grease.

MY SWEET WIFE
HE MET THIS YOUNG GIRL TWENTY
SOME YEARS AGO. HE FELL
IN LOVE WITH HER VERY DEEPLY
AND STILL LOVES HER VERY, VERY
MUCH. FOR MANY YEARS HE WAS
TOO INTO HIMSELF AND HIS DRINKS
AND HE HURT HER OFTEN AND
PAINFULLY AND HE IS VERY SORRY.
HE FEELS HE IS VERY LUCKY TO
STILL HAVE THIS WONDERFUL
PERSON WITH HIM. LAST NIGHT HE
LAYED IN BED AND CRIED, HE HAD
SEEN HOW SAD SHE WAS THAT HER
CLOSE LOVED ONES HAD PAID SO
LITTLE ATTENTION TO HER BIRTHDAY.
HER HUSBAND DID NOT EVEN BUY HER
A CARD. AGAIN HE IS SORRY, AGAIN
THIS MORNING HE CRIED. HE LOVES
THIS PRETTY LADY OH SO MUCH BUT
HE HAS A VERY POOR WAY OF SHOWING
IT. HER LOVES MUST FIND A WAY TO MAKE
HER HAPPY. WE NEED HER, SHE IS IM-
POSSIBLE TO REPLACE. AGAIN HE IS SORRY.
               I love you,
               Lowell (L.P.)

P.S. HE HOPES IN A WEEK OR TWO HE CAN TAKE HER AWAY FOR A WEEKEND AND LET HER RELAX AND ENJOY HERSELF AND HAVE HER L.P. GET TO SPEAK TO HER FOR A CHANGE. FOR HER BIRTHDAY HER HUSBAND WILL TRY TO BE THE HUSBAND HE SHOULD BE.

I wished I could respect the man who had written this letter, especially since I recognized how flawed and imperfect we all were. I wished I could report that my father had seen the error of his ways and changed, but there were simply too many of them—all apologies, all oddly formal and stilted and full of a flowery, overwrought sentimentality that belied true emotion. Who wrote an apology note in the third person? Was it so hard to say "I'm sorry" that he had to distance himself as "he" in a simple handwritten note? And who referred to his own wife as "this pretty lady"? The part that killed me was the PS, where he "hopes" to take my mother away for a weekend and "let her enjoy herself and have her L.P. get to speak to her for a change"—as if it was such a luxury, such a treat, such an extremely special occasion for a husband to talk to his wife.

Of course, the special weekend never happened. There were many promised and few delivered. I remembered my mother crying about these missed birthdays and broken promises, and how amazed I was, even as a young child, by the way she could cry with so much rage. I wanted to comfort her; God knows I tried. I learned that I mustn't do anything to upset her, because she already had so much worry in her life that there wasn't room for any more. I played quietly; I read books; I did not ask for anything I knew we couldn't afford, because I'd certainly learned my lesson with that one.

Once I'd asked for a really cool pair of green suede sneakers with gold trim up at John's Shoe Box, the shoe store connected to my father's barber shop. My little red corduroy rubber-toed sneakers had seen better days. But everyone in the fifth grade was wearing Pumas and certainly no one was wearing corduroy sneakers. But when I'd asked, my mother had sighed so deeply that it seemed to take all the air out of the room. She'd put down her embroidery hoop, sticking the needle through the top while she paused to deal with me. "You know I can't afford that right now," she said. "Dad doesn't get paid until next Friday. Your red shoes are fine. They're cute."

I rarely did this, but I remember pushing a little, begging this time. "But please," I whined. "I really, really, really want them. I never get anything new!"

It was just enough to set her off. "Jesus Christ!" she said. "I said, no. Why can't you understand that? I can't pull money from the sky, you know." She huffed and went to pour herself a glass of Pepsi. She always drank Pepsi to soothe herself. I can still hear the psst of the bottle opening, the clink of ice in the glass, then the fizzy sound of the soda tumbling over, crackling the ice.

Now that I was a parent myself, the idea of being unable to afford new shoes for your child nearly crushed me with anguish for what my mother must've experienced in those moments. And even though it was always her on the front lines with us, saying yes or no, managing and refereeing us through the worst, I knew the truth. I knew the source of all this pain: my father. He'd come home swaying and tilting, smiling. He'd try to open the refrigerator, stumble, laugh, and say something like, "Whoopsie-doodle, there!" He'd make a gesture to put his arm around my mother, but she'd sidestep him without saying a word.

My mother's grimace would be so tight, her movements so clipped and cold as she stuck another frozen pizza in the oven for dinner (for six), I could almost see the negative ions zigzagging through the air.

Some notes from my father revealed their unspoken context. My father, a true addict, had a fondness for scratch-off lottery tickets as well as the casino. This was always a sore spot between him and my mother, as he often lost all of their money that way. One note read: *Did you know I think you get more beautiful each day? You know I lost some money yesterday, but next time it's gonna be big! Just wait. Later, love you, Me.* Another roundabout apology that I could imagine all too clearly. Despite their mountain of bills and paltry paychecks, my father couldn't resist the idea of "what if": what if he really won big? He claimed that he'd quit his job that very minute and sleep all day. My mother, who worked various minimum wage jobs, was the one who had to worry over their precarious finances. She'd beg him not to gamble, which usually resulted in the loss of most of his paycheck; you simply couldn't tell my dad what to do.

Another note revealed the jealousy my father always felt about my mother having such a rich social life. She had two close female friends, and also a great relationship with her two sisters, Sandy and Beth. One note I found from him read: *My darling wife. I'm sorry about what I said. I'm glad you and Beth went out—it's good for you. I love you more every day. Love, Me.* I knew this argument well, since my mother complained about it to me so often I could almost recite the exact lines.

My mother, as she'd report it to me: "Just because your dad never wants to go out and do anything, he expects me to sit around the house all the time while he ignores me. But I like to go out! I like getting in the mix! All he wants to do is lay around and sleep and groan about how tired he is but then when I make plans to do something with my own sister, he gets all bucky! He's worse than a little kid. Well, I just told him I'm sick of it already and I'm just going. But then he punishes me and guilt trips me when I get back."

Sadly, it was true. Even when my mother came to visit me in New York, my father was mean-spirited about it—though he was always invited as well. "I just can't get myself on an airplane," he'd say, wringing his hands together. "I get so anxious. And then I can't breathe. I'd have to go to the doc and get a prescription for something, but even then, I just don't think I can do it." So my mother would scrimp and save, buy a ticket and come out to see us. It didn't happen often, but when it did, it was a blast. She was a great traveler, always up for anything. But when she'd call to check in with my dad, the storm clouds gathered.

He'd go off to the casino while she was in New York, his passive-aggressive way of punishing her for leaving him alone. He'd blow all their money, which made her worried and guilty about spending so much on the trip in the first place, which dampened the rest of the trip, even when I'd offer to pay for everything.

"Your dad can be such a..."—but she wouldn't finish. Despite his emotionally abusive behavior, she still felt a need to protect and defend him to us kids. "He's just...ach, who cares?" She'd throw her hands up in the air in a gesture of fake nonchalance. "Let's just go have ourselves a good time." But as we ate Buffalo wings, or browsed through Lift Bridge Book Shop, I could see the dents of worry in her forehead as she eyed prices and minded her wallet.

Here's the thing: my father was not a terrible person. Most everyone who knew him loved him and thought he was hilarious.

He could shoot the shit with people in town, with strangers, with his AA buddies, with his siblings. But that was exactly the problem: put him with his very own wife, his very own children, and he grew silent. He withdrew from us like a rabbit burrows into its hole—as if the idea of us and our desperate needy hearts posed a danger to him, as if we might eat him alive—when all we really wanted was his simple presence.

One last letter from my father to my mother caught my eye. It was longer than most of the others and written on actual stationery.

Babs,
Many times as I sit around the house when I am not working, be it on weekends
or mornings, when we are home together, it may seem that I do not say much to
you and I am being a buck to you. It is not always the case. I still often keep
things to myself and use silence to cover my being upset or things that get
to me. I want to tell you how I really feel about you. I want you happy.
ME

One Saturday morning, the kids and I get ready to go biking. It's almost ninety degrees outside and it's not even noon.

There are two large puddles in the middle of our driveway from last night's storm. As Lily cruises through one of them, she says, "Look! There's a dragonfly in there!" And sure enough, when I bend down to check, there's a dragonfly on its back, bicycling its legs, struggling to pull itself out.

"Let's try to save it," I say. I take hold of its slender torso, gently shake some of the water off it, and then place it, feet down, on the hot pavement. It doesn't move. The kids begin to bike in circles again while I stand guard by the wet, possibly dead dragonfly.

I crouch beside it and blow on its wings. "Maybe when its wings dry off, it'll be able to fly again," I tell the kids as they zoom around me.

"Yeah," they say.

I watch as the dragonfly twirls its head around. Its face is tan—black dots for eyes. Its gossamer wings blend right into the pavement.

The kids swerve dangerously close to each other and almost crash. While I'm yelling at them to be careful, somehow I lose sight of the dragonfly.

"It flew away," Lily says. "It went over there." She points up to the sky but I see nothing. I was ready to scoop it up in my hands, blow-dry its wings, nurse it back to health.

Lily looks up at the sky nervously.

"It's all right," I say. "She was probably just passing by for a quick visit."

One of the benefits of being a college professor is that every seven years, if you keep up with your scholarship, you become eligible for a semester's paid sabbatical leave to work on your next project. For my first sabbatical, after numerous discussions about where we should go, Mark applied for a Fulbright fellowship to Vietnam; he would teach and I would write my next book. Having met and lived in the Philippines, we were both drawn to southeast Asia; plus, we absolutely loved Vietnamese food, joking that pho noodles were one of the main reasons we picked Vietnam. When Mark found out he'd recieved the fellowship, we were thrilled. Our kids were still little (Lily was two and Hudson five) and would get to experience a foreign culture and maybe even pick up the Vietnamese language.

When I'd called my mother to tell her we were all moving to Vietnam for six months, there was dead silence.

"Mom?" I asked. "Are you still there?" I could hear the television mumbling in the background. My mother loved to watch Martha Stewart in the mornings while she drank her coffee. I could imagine her sitting in the den in her pink fleece robe, their cat, Kiki, on her lap and her latest quilting project draped over her legs. She'd known for months that Mark had applied for the Fulbright, but I think she chose to ignore it.

"Hmm," she said. "So what brought this on?"

"Well," I said, even though we'd gone through this a thousand times before. "Remember I told you he applied last year? He just found out he got it! So we get to go abroad for our sabbatical. Isn't that great?"

"Oh, yeah," she said, as if it were everyday news to be moving to Vietnam. But there was a pinch of worry in her nonchalance; I could hear it. "And what about the kids?"

I knew the kids' safety was her main concern, but I wanted her to understand we weren't doing this recklessly, but for reasons that were important to us. "Well, for starters, we want Hudson and Lily to see the world."

We lived in western New York, and although Brockport was a college town, it was also politically conservative and religiously fervent. It wasn't uncommon to pass anti-abortion protesters while driving to the Wegmans grocery store, or to encounter fundamentalist Christians on the sidewalk, proselytizing about the need to be saved before the Rapture. Plus, although we liked Hudson's kindergarten teacher, we noticed little by little that Hudson had come home singing "You're a Grand Old Flag" and the Marines' Hymn.

"Well, there's nothing wrong with being patriotic," my mother said. She and my father had a giant American flag in their front yard with petunias surrounding it in summer. They flew the flag daily, long before the patriotic frenzy inspired by 9/11 began.

"No, there isn't," I said, but I could feel my voice tighten. "It's just that we want them to understand other perspectives, too. Other points of view."

"Uh-huh," she said. Subtext: can we please talk about something else? "So, where exactly are you going to live in Vietnam?"

"Can Tho," I said. "I'm looking at it right now online." It was smack in the middle of the Mekong Delta, just about the hottest place you could live in Vietnam. I tried to describe some Google images of Can Tho to her: a muddy confluence of rivers, rickety wooden boats crowding the water, tin shacks on stilts overhanging the Mekong River. Although neither Mark nor I had ever heard of it, Can Tho was Vietnam's third-largest city, with a population of 1.5 million.

Mark and I had researched everything we could about Can Tho, and had discovered it was called Vietnam's "bread basket" because of all the food that was grown there. It was the last city to surrender to the North Vietnamese Army in 1975. It had a thriving snake market. It was about three hours south of Saigon. I shared these tidbits with my mother.

"And get this," I said to her. "The average daily temperature is 97 degrees, and the humidity level is roughly the same." We were Minnesotans, after all, and loved weather talk.

"Oh my God!" she said. "I could never stand that. How are you going to stand that? I'd never make it there."

The fact was, heat or no heat, travel was not something my family did. My mother lived right next door to her childhood home. She knew everyone in Arlington, and it sometimes pained me to go run errands with her when I went home to visit. She'd have to stop and talk to Lorraine, the bank teller, about their friend Marcia's surgery; she would chat with Les, the pharmacist at Rexall Drug, about his new lake cabin "up north." She was on her class reunion planning committee and had married her high school sweetheart, my father, who'd grown up just seven miles away in the town of Green Isle, population 336. Part, or most, of the reason they didn't travel was because they lacked money and vacation time. Plus, they worked so hard that when they did get time off, they claimed that all they wanted to do was stay home, putter around the yard, rent movies, and sleep.

"So what do the kids think about all of this?" she asked.

"They're excited," I said. "Lily doesn't really get it, but Hudson thinks it's cool. His kindergarten class is throwing a big going-away party for him." I conveniently left out the part about Hudson's occasional tears and his worries about how Santa and the Easter Bunny would find him in Vietnam. "Oh," I added, "we're also going to start a blog. Hudson's excited about that."

"Huh," my mother said.

The fact was, I'd lived far away from my parents for most of my adult life. The very day after my high school graduation, I left home to work as an actress in a summer repertory theater company. Somehow it never hit me before how hard that must've been for my mother when she dropped me off; I was seventeen and had never so much as fried an egg for myself or kept a checkbook, yet there I was moving into an apartment with a bunch of actors who smoked, dyed their hair jet black, and wore bandanas tied around their jeans. Then there was the fact of my joining the Peace Corps right after college: two years in the Philippines without even a phone call. I remembered her red-rimmed eyes at the airport when I left.

"Don't worry," I told my mother. "We'll be careful. Plus, we'll post lots of pictures on the blog so you can see how well the kids are doing."

"Well, good," she said. I heard her yawn. "I should probably get going. I've got to go set Grandma's hair. She always thinks it has to be done every Tuesday morning at nine o'clock on the dot. As if she's on a real tight schedule."

I used to love sitting at my grandma's kitchen table while my mother set my grandma's hair. Polka music would be playing on the radio, and the coffee percolator would bubble on the stove, filling the room with the rich scent of Folgers. My grandma would sit with a towel clutched around her neck while my mother applied Dippity Do to each section, then rolled them up tight in pink scratchy curlers with a white plastic stick poked through. My mother always complained about doing this, but I think that she secretly enjoyed it as much as I did.

After my mother and I said goodbye and promised to talk soon, I realized I hadn't asked her how she was feeling, nor had she given me any health updates. We usually spent a good portion of our phone calls catching up on her latest doctor visits and health problems, and the lack of it this time made me wonder if perhaps things were on the upswing. It'd been a year since her second bladder repair surgery, and though I knew she still didn't feel great, maybe, just maybe, I thought, she was getting better.

Lake Minnewawa

One of the few places our family ever traveled was to my grandparents' cabin on Lake Minnewawa in McGregor, Minnesota. It wasn't much of a town, but it did have a Dairy Queen, as well as Sather's store, where we'd stop for groceries before going to the cabin. I would save up my babysitting money all year so I could buy *Seventeen*, *Vogue*, and *Mademoiselle* magazines, as well as a Lake Minnewawa sweatshirt with raised white letters and a big walleye on the front.

The cabin was painted pale green with white scalloped trim. Inside, the walls were dark knotty pine, and the layout was simple: a combined kitchen and living room in front, and in the back, a bathroom flanked by two small bedrooms. I loved pushing open the door and sucking in that musty, wood-smoke smell. My favorite thing was helping my mother settle into the cabin, putting the groceries and our toiletries away. We didn't travel often, and I found great pleasure in arranging our toothpaste and toothbrushes on the beveled glass shelf in the bathroom.

The traditions never changed: cherry Kool-Aid, Old Dutch potato chips, Kemp's Butter Brickle ice cream, mosquito coils smoking on top of an old Mountain Dew glass bottle. During the day, we fought over who got to sit in the coveted pink chaise lounge under the birch tree, and at night we watched the low-budget news station from Duluth and made fun of the hairdos and clothing.

My father always vanished immediately to fish off of the dock, and as soon as he did, I could feel my mother settle into herself and relax. To be away from her difficult life back in the trailer court, to breathe in the scent of pine trees and hot dogs on the grill, must have been such a welcome change for her. Plus, whenever my grandparents would join us, which they often did, I got to see my mother being taken care of and served. When my grandma asked, "Who wants eggs and how would you like them?" my mother replied, "Oh, I'll take some scrambled, please. Thanks." Then she'd sit back with her *Better Homes and Gardens*, leafing through it idly while wiggling her freshly painted toenails on the footstool. This was not my usual mother.

Up at the cabin we could all pretend, at least for a weekend, that we, too, were a happy, wholesome middle-class family on vacation. No one knew we lived in a trailer court. No one knew we got free lunch tickets at school because we were so poor. No one knew my father dry-heaved over the toilet, hung over, almost every morning. We were just like the hearty, happy family next door who played Monopoly on the front porch, then later went zooming off in their speedboat, their laughter echoing across the lake.

When my grandparents didn't join us, however, we fell into our old habits pretty quickly. My father was never without a beer in his hand, and my mother, as he continued to get drunker and stay out on the dock longer and longer, started talking angrily through clenched teeth. She'd yell at us when we asked her to intervene in a particularly contentious game of Sorry, or resisted her efforts to put us to bed, or complained that the hot dogs had too much black on them. "I don't care!" she'd say. "And apparently neither does your father since he thinks he can do whatever the hell he wants while I have to sit here and figure out meals and clean everything up and deal with all of you kids fighting nonstop. Jesus!"

Invariably, she asked one of us to go down to the dock and get him. I remember walking carefully down the steps, then standing on the warm dock in bare feet, my father nowhere in sight. With a hand over my eyes, I scanned the lake, paying special attention to the reedy patches where I knew the fish bit. I could barely make my father out in the distance; I could tell it was him by the lazy cast of his line and an occasional quick head movement as he tipped back a beer. Going back to report that my father was out of earshot and would therefore not be back for a long time was hard.

My siblings and I soon learned the drill: stay out of our mother's way. We spent almost all of our time down in the lake. We took turns with two black inner tubes and two air mattresses, and I spent hours floating out there on the water in a near dream state.

"Okay," Amy said. She often ended up on one of the air mattresses, which always developed a slow leak. "Pretend you're lost out at sea in that inner tube and I'm a big ship that goes by and you try to get my attention to come save you." Amy had a short blonde pixie for many years, and when she spent so much time in the sun, it turned pure white.

"Nah," I said. "That's dumb." I trailed my fingertips through the water.

My brother, Jim, liked to dig up leeches along the shoreline and scare us with them. He threw a leech my direction. It plopped in the water like a rock.

"You missed!" I said, then got back to my tanning. Sometimes I stuck a little square of masking tape on my stomach to mark my progress.

Then, as I was floating along in my inner tube, I felt something on my leg. I peeked underneath my sunglasses and saw a dragonfly on my thigh. "Oh my God!" I yelled. "Look at this!" Of course, it flew away, startled, but when I propped myself up, I noticed several of them droning about, flitting from one place to another, often landing on the water for the briefest of moments.

"Do they bite?" Amy said. She took after my mother's side of the family; she couldn't take as much sun as the rest of us, and her skin grew pink quickly. "I think they bite!"

"They don't bite," Jim said. He was pulling our younger brother, Mike, around in a blue plastic boat the size of a bathtub. It had been at the cabin for as long as I could remember. "They're nice. They eat mosquitoes."

I watched another one land on my inner tube, right next to my hand. I barely breathed, marveling at its gauzy, iridescent wings. Its long cobalt blue body remained perfectly still, but I could see its compound eyes moving around, watching us.

Jim threw another leech at me and it landed on my arm.

Of course, the dragonfly flew away.

One of the things I inherited from my mother was her high school yearbooks. When I opened *The 1963 Indian*, some of the pages stuck or ripped apart with age. The very first page featured a photo of the whole senior class sitting at library tables, waving. It was a deep, wide-angle shot, and many people were barely visible, but there in black and white was my mother, front and center. She wore a pale fitted dress she had most likely sewn herself. It was elegant with a notched waist, bust and waist darts, and three-quarter-length sleeves. One of her legs was slightly tilted to the side, showing, possibly on purpose, her lovely, slender calves. She wore modest black heels and a gold necklace. How perfectly elegant, what gorgeous bone structure, such grace, except that she was looking off to the side in a way that clouded her smile a bit. While everyone else's happiness looked pure, unreserved, and hopeful, there was a nervous little twist in her face that suggested uncertainty.

Had she perhaps seen a future ghost of herself trapped in a horrible marriage to an alcoholic, emotionally distant husband? Had she seen flashes of her life in the trailer court with no money and no working car? And had it scared her momentarily, but not quite enough for her to run screaming in the other direction?

I'd never know.

And yet, I did know: she hadn't seen it coming.

I knew this because during the few times I got her to talk about why she'd married my father, she always said the same thing. When I asked, "Why did you marry him if he was already an alcoholic, even in high school?" her answer was: "I thought I could change him."

Of course she did.

But this seemed too simplistic to me for someone as smart as my mother was. Listed underneath her senior photo, her credits included the National Honor Society, the Quill and Scroll Club, the International Society of High School Journalists, the yearbook staff, the Tom-Tom staff, and many others. How could she have cast all that aside for such an uncertain life with my father? Didn't anyone try to warn her? But then, I reminded myself, it was 1963. Getting married was what girls did. Plus, she'd been just eighteen years old—*eighteen*—and the first one in her class to "have a rock on her finger," according to many of the senior calling cards she kept in a shoebox. Scribbled on the back of the tiny cards were comments that spoke of her engagement with an almost reverential awe.

Dear Barb, Will never forget you for being in English class but most of all for having that ring on your finger and future plans with Lowell Panning. Best of luck.
—Rollie.

Barbara, I won't forget the most popular girl in our class. Also, your artistic abilities, sense of humor, and for the big engagement.
—Mike.

Barb, You have so many wonderful qualities that I'll remember about you, esp. for being the senior girl with the diamond.
—Betty.

Barb, Will remember you for that dazzling rock on your finger.
—Mary

Barb, how could I forget someone who goes with Lowell P?
—Ray

Despite his budding alcoholism, my father was tall, athletic, and good-looking. And by all accounts, he was funny, exerting a magnetic pull that drew others to him effortlessly. According to one of my uncles, my father started the Bermuda-shorts-wearing trend in Arlington, long before it hit the rest of Minnesota. Who wouldn't be lured in by such a guy?

By the time my mother was a senior in high school, my father had already been out of school for two years; that January, he was accepted to Lee's School of Barbering in St. Paul, where he studied scalp diseases, hair product chemistry, face and scalp massage, and how to shave with a straight-edge razor. My Aunt Beth reported to me how proud my mother had been of this fact. It was a profession, something respectable that required textbooks and training. Of course, in the early sixties, going to college had not yet become the assumed path for most high school seniors that it was now. Plus, neither of my father's parents had gone to college; in fact, my Grandpa Panning never completed more than an eighth-grade education, though he clearly had the brains and acumen to later run his own business—Panning's Town & Country Store—alongside my grandma, a shrewd businesswoman with a high school diploma. I was sure it had never crossed my father's mind that he might've been college material. But hadn't it crossed my mother's? Her mother had studied to be a nurse in St. Paul; she'd been an educated city girl. My mother's father, never without a *National Geographic* in hand, an atlas and a magnifying lens nearby, wanted to be a doctor, but his family could only afford to send one child to college—his older brother—leaving my grandpa to start a career as a butter maker.

My mother should've gone to college. If she'd come of age just a couple decades later, I liked to think she most certainly would've. Recently, I found some of her old journalism papers from high school, all with big red *As* gracing the top. She had a sure and confident style, especially for someone so young.

I found one very short piece entitled "Little Spectators."

While watching the New Prague game last Wednesday night, I noticed a little bird sitting on the playing field watching the game, too. It looked like a little wren. He was more on our side of the field, and seemed to be rooting for our team. I hope he wasn't too disappointed that we lost. I didn't see him fly away. Maybe he's still sitting there.

There was something about this piece I admired. On one level, it was an anecdote without much analysis or reflection. But on another level, it was poetic, almost existential in its brevity and understatement. She couldn't have been more than seventeen years old when she'd written it, but as someone who taught college-level writing, I was impressed by the maturity of the voice, the sensitivity to the world that's expressed, the economical language used. She got a "B+" on it.

Another piece, "4th Hour Growl—Cha, Cha, Cha," showed her sense of humor.

A new, but then again, maybe not so new, dance craze is sweeping our school. It might be called a sit-down version of the Twist, but instead of being called a Twister, the person doing the 4th Hour Growl is called "a downright breakfast-skipper."

She then went on with this conceit to list the "basic steps" of the dance—skipping breakfast, the "itty bitty pain way down in your tummy-tum-tum," after which "you hear the whale of a growl and you're ready to begin!"

Yes, there was a preponderance of exclamation points. Yes, it was corny and more than a little clunky, but I was thrilled to find evidence of this playful, literary version of my mother.

All these years I'd thought of my mother and me as polar opposites: she was a homebody, a quilter and seamstress. I was a traveler, a writer and professor. Her goals were modest; I was doggedly ambitious. But maybe we weren't so different after all. We both created. We both aspired to make something of beauty where there was none. We both loved words.

Another journalism paper she'd written was ungraded, and unlike the others, it was written in pencil.

Journalism, I feel, has been a very worthwhile course, and I can honestly say that it has been my favorite course. Unlike many subjects, it gives one a chance to participate in the actual goings-on of the world and not just day after day of reading—things like the trip to the *Arlington Enterprise* office, the *Star and Tribune* offices in Minneapolis, the putting out of the *Tom Tom*, have helped me so to understand the <u>art</u> of writing and publishing. I honestly feel that it's helped me in putting down my thoughts and feelings on paper in an effective way, even if it's something I put away in my desk, and no one else ever sees it. My only gripe about Journalism is that it's over.

My mother had always been a reader. She kept stacks of paperbacks by her bedside, and I remember that she was such a frequent patron of the library that she literally wore out her card. But I hadn't known how much writing had piqued her interest until finding these high school papers in her cedar chest.

Then, as I was organizing her papers in a folder labeled "MOM'S WRITING," a small yellowed newspaper clipping fluttered out of the pile. I picked it up and read the headline: "Hands: a Sonnet by Barbara Griep." It was like someone had thrown a bucket of water into my face. How could I not have known about this? Not just a poem but a *sonnet*? Writing a sonnet was serious business. It took time, expertise, attention to beat and sound and meter. Who but an aspiring writer would attempt to write something as difficult as a sonnet? Why had she never shared this with me, her English-major daughter and aspiring writer?

I made copies to send to my siblings, but wondered if they'd be as excited as I was. And then, not sure what to do with this poem on such aged, fragile paper, I decided I had to frame it. Immediately. As if it might disintegrate if I didn't act right away.

I bought a 1940s frame in a dark green fern print, and the poem looked perfect when I placed it inside. I read the sonnet again and suddenly I made an odd connection. One summer, years earlier, when I'd been visiting my parents in Minnesota, I'd had my old 35mm Pentax with me. I'd been hatching an idea for a photo project: a close-up of every family member's left hand, in black and white, against the rough faded wood of the picnic table. Though my brothers thought it was kind of odd my mother kept saying how wrinkly and "icky" her hands looked, everyone cooperated. Later, I had all of the hand photographs matted and framed and it became one of my most treasured possessions: my father's hand, grease-grimed and gnarly from hard labor; my mother's, soft, pale, slightly puffy with a slim wedding band; my sister's, strong and friendly; my own hand almost identical to my mother's; my two brothers', darkly suntanned from construction work—all of them, so recognizably them. I looked at our six hands all tucked neatly inside the frame, and realized they suggested a truer sense of us than any portrait could.

I hung my mother's framed sonnet next to it.

There are hands that are gnarled, cut, and torn,
By sweet and hard labor they are worn.

Back in my study, I looked at all the things she'd saved, the things she'd written. Her words, these objects, weren't random anymore, not silly heaps of a high school girl's memorabilia, but prophecies cast out as constellations to light my way.

Moving two children under the age of five to Vietnam wasn't easy. Luckily, Mark and I weren't opposed to using bribery as an effective motivational tool. Getting Lily to sit through a haircut, for example, could be easily accomplished by offering a Tootsie Pop after the blow-dry. Hudson could be cajoled into making his bed by letting him watch *Tom and Jerry* episodes back to back. So, after dragging them both on a nearly thirty-hour, three-layover, eleven-time-zone airplane ride, we knew there had to be something good waiting for them on the other side—e.g. a decent place to live. Unfortunately, with no vehicle, no comprehension of the Vietnamese language, and no time to spare, our first task was finding a house to rent. Allegedly, one of Mark's colleagues at Can Tho University had agreed to help us, but we hadn't heard anything yet and didn't even know his name, much less how to reach him.

We'd reserved a hotel room for six days, and from its window we could see the muddy Mekong River bustling with boat traffic. Clusters of rusty tin shacks clung to the shore, held up by wooden stilts sunk into the water below. Tarps and towels served as doors and windows, and bright clothing dried on bamboo poles hung over the water like flags.

A haze of humidity hovered visibly over the horizon. Can Tho was still a fairly undeveloped tourist destination, although there was a small group of people lined up for the next Floating Market tour—Can Tho's one claim to fame. All over the river, boats clustered together, some filled with pineapples, others with flats of bottled water; others contained whole families dressed neatly for work and school, and some even managed to cook noodles and rice on small wood-burning stoves at the rear of the boats.

Eager to let the kids blow off some steam, we headed to the Ninh Kie Quay, a small riverfront park with a tiny green lawn and an enormous statue of Ho Chi Minh at its center. It was a pleasant green oasis from the loud, frantic traffic blasting around us. We let the kids run back and forth across the grass and work off some of their energy. Mark and I laughed as they started climbing up Ho Chi Minh, but we were immediately tapped on the shoulder by a soldier in a crisp olive green uniform. He pointed to a sign, written in Vietnamese, and nodded toward the children. We had no clue. Was the park closed? Were we supposed to pay to use it? The fact that he was armed with an AK-47 was not comforting.

Fortunately, a young Vietnamese college student came to our rescue. "The rule is no one to enter the proximity to Ho Chi Minh. And no touch." She pointed to the kids scrambling onto his huge stone legs. We quickly called them down and explained that the statue was off limits. Lily cried and said she was hot; her little ponytails were wet with sweat. Hudson said his stomach hurt, which we knew meant he was hungry, so we thanked the girl and headed down the street to look for a place to eat.

A teenaged boy beckoned us into a restaurant, and, like all the shops in Vietnam, it had no fourth wall. As we sat there trying to order, motorcycles zoomed up right next to us. I could feel the hot exhaust radiating against my bare legs when they came too close.

Since one of the reasons we'd chosen to go to Vietnam was the food, we were both excited for our first real Vietnamese meal.

We loved hot, comforting bowls of pho, lemongrass chicken with fresh vegetables on cold rice vermicelli noodles, and fresh shrimp rolls dipped in chili-peanut sauce.

Of course, once faced with actually ordering in Vietnam, things became much more difficult. Most everything was in Vietnamese, and even when there were English translations, meanings were unclear. *Rurality Salad. Soup with sport in Cucumber. Pork with Fresh Garbage.* We did our best to order, but once our food arrived—a gluey-eyed gray fish bathed in a pale orange sauce—it was hard to eat, even for Mark and me. The kids ate rice with soy sauce.

"We really need to find a place to live," I said to Mark. "Where we can cook."

"Totally," Mark said. He yanked a milky chunk off the fish carcass with chopsticks. "The sooner, the better."

We looked at nine houses in a span of six days. One came with an albino pit bull that acted like it wanted to eat our children. One was a tall, skinny house in the middle of a field that apparently came with a family of six. I fell in love with a pink house with two air-conditioned bedrooms, only to discover it was attached to a discotheque next door. Finally, one of Mark's university colleagues, Khanh, showed up, out of the blue, and within twenty-four hours, we found a place.

Once we got set up, we posted photos of the house on our blog, because I knew my mother would be worried sick if she didn't see physical evidence of us, the kids, and a solid place to live. Amazingly, despite her computer-challenged ways, she commented on the blog post almost immediately. "Amy is here helping us. We think we got it. We are so thrilled to see your photos and to know all is well. We love you and miss you! Mom and Dad."

The speed of her response made me realize how worried she really was. She knew Mark and I were savvy travelers, but the idea of taking the kids caused her great anxiety. Lily was, after all, only two years old and still in diapers.

As I kept a record of our new experiences on our blog, I gradually learned to censor what I posted, primarily for my mother's benefit. Once, when someone had broken into our house and stolen my credit card, I'd (quite stupidly) blogged about it. Even from across the globe, I could practically hear my mother's accusatory chiding. "Didn't I tell you to be careful over there? What about the kids? Next thing you know someone will be trying to snatch them away, too! I told you not to go somewhere like Vietnam. Why couldn't you just go somewhere nice and normal like England or Ireland where it's safe and people speak English? I'm never gonna sleep now I'll be so worried about those two little kids over there."

And so I began to blog about only pleasant anecdotes and experiences ("Absolutely love the way the Vietnamese adore our children here—they're treated like royalty!" or "Check out this amazing pedicure I got last week—for just $1.50 U.S.!"). As time wore on, however, I began to feel disconnected and lonely in a way I'd never felt before while abroad. Maybe it was having the kids to tend to all day and not much interaction beyond that. Maybe it was the way our tiny lane dead-ended and isolated us. I felt a strong tug of nostalgia for my hometown and my family in Minnesota. I missed my mother. I missed my sister. I lived for their brief, occasional responses to my blog posts, and found myself disappointed when days passed without hearing from them.

Of course, I knew that everyone in my family was busy working, that they didn't have the free time we had in Vietnam.

But still. It seemed I'd always craved more from my family than they were able to give. My parents, especially, seemed to live from one precarious moment to the next, often with their lack of money creating miniature traumas and tensions on a daily basis. Even though I was thousands of miles away, I longed for their constant contact.

Eventually, I had an epiphany: if I wanted to be in such close contact with my family, then surely I wouldn't have moved to someplace as far away as Vietnam (or the Philippines or Hawaii or New York or Ohio or Idaho or China). Right?

This fact, however obvious, eluded me in its simplicity.

Between April and July 2007, scientists discover four new species of dragonflies on Phu Quoc island in Vietnam.

In April 2007, Mark and I rent a beach bungalow on Phu Quoc with Hudson and Lily for a week. Though I see plenty of Phu Quoc ridgeback dogs running wild through ditches, I don't see a single dragonfly. Even when we spend an afternoon inland, visiting a fish sauce factory surrounded by freshwater streams and rivers, I don't see any dragonflies.

Only later will I learn that during the time we were there, scientists toiled away in thick tropical forests, gathering new and never-seen-before dragonflies. One of them, *Lyriothemis mortoni*, was gorgeous and unusual with a powder-blue thorax and an amber-tipped abdomen that looked exactly like the orange glowing end of a cigarette.

In July 2007, after entomologists wrap up their survey on Phu Quoc island and head home, my mother dies in Minnesota.

At the time I'm not looking for dragonflies.

Not yet.

Mother's Day

One of my favorite things to do in Vietnam was shop at the fabric market. Even though I could barely thread a needle, I felt a great connection to my mother when I was surrounded by fabric. I could spend hours fingering through bolts of brightly printed cotton and rich, jeweled-toned silk, trying to imagine how it would look as a dress or a skirt. I loved to hunt for just the right buttons and zippers and "notions" like my mother and I used to do at Hartmann's in Arlington.

Hartmann's was primarily a clothing store, but there was a room in back with big metal cabinets full of Simplicity patterns. My mother and I would often settle in, searching first for the right pattern, then selecting the perfect fabric from the ninety-nine-cent table. To this day, there's nothing more comforting or more hopeful to me than the sound of cloth cut fresh off the bolt: the soft thud as it's laid upon the table, the crisp metallic opening of the scissors, the definitive chop into the fabric, and finally the last soft pats of cloth as it's folded into quarters.

In Vietnam, I had no trouble finding fabric I loved, but finding someone to sew things for me was challenging because of the language barrier. Luckily, one of Mark's colleagues helped me find a wonderful tailor. Her name was Ngan, and though she spoke no English, her aunt next door, Ms. Loan, was a teacher and was happy to translate.

One day I went to Ngan's with a plastic bag full of fabric and a head full of ideas.

Ngan and I sat on the floor of her "shop" (i.e., living room). It was a tiny space with a very low ceiling, a sewing machine shoved in one corner, and garments in mid-completion hanging on nails all over the walls.

While I tried to explain what I wanted done, Ngan rubbed my arm with her hand, which felt soft, warm, and buttery. I was sweating like I'd run a marathon, and she graciously handed me a wet-wipe packet, ubiquitous in Vietnam. *"Cam on,"* I said, one of the few Vietnamese phrases I'd mastered. *Thank you.*

I wanted a pair of silk pajamas with a matching robe, a gored panel knee-length skirt, and an empire-waist dress with a gathered neckline. Ngan fingered the fabric approvingly, then spun me around and made me raise my sweaty armpits while she slowly measured every inch of me. She smelled like mothballs; she wore tiny glasses and I could see when I peeked at her how smudged they were. "Mmm," she kept saying. "Hmm." I had to admit I liked the feeling of her touch—it was firm, warm, and purposeful. I could clearly remember my mother's fingertips holding thin tissue paper pattern pieces up against my body— the feeling of warmth mixed with the crunch of the delicate paper.

I loved being in Ngan's little shop, and knew much of this had to do with my mother. For years my mother had her sewing machine set up on the dining room table, and I loved sitting there with a cup of coffee while she held pins between her teeth and fed material through the machine, the foot pedal pushing it along. If she didn't get it exactly right, she'd pull the whole thing apart and insist on doing it all over again. Those moments with her—John Denver playing on her cassette player, the cats weaving back and forth between our legs, the hum of her machine zipping through cotton—brought us together in a way nothing else did.

When Ngan and I ran out of body language, Ms. Loan came in to save us. She spoke wonderful English and helped clear up any confusion before a piece was sewn. I loved spending time with them. Ms. Loan had tons of questions about American idioms and culture. One day she asked what it meant when someone said they were crazy about someone. Another day she wanted to know what parasailing was. "And what is the meaning of 'to butter someone up'?" she asked me one day, and I had a very difficult time explaining that clearly.

One day, Ms. Loan invited me, yet again, to join her on Sunday mornings for English Club. Ever since I'd met her, she'd been hounding me to come to the club as her guest and wouldn't seem to take no for an answer.

"Plus, Annie, I believe your American holiday Mother's Day is approaching," Ms. Loan said. Her enormous eyes grew even bigger behind tinted lenses. "You should join us for this Mother's Day next Sunday. We will celebrate you!"

She was so convincing, and had asked me so many times, that I finally acquiesced. "Well, okay," I said.

The topic of discussion for that week's English Club was what constitutes happiness.

The club leader prodded me to begin by asking me what constitutes the American Dream. "You will tell us, Miss Panning, what are the components of this American Dream."

"Well, you work hard," I said, "and you get married, have children, buy a house and car, go on some nice vacations, send your kids to college, then save up for retirement." It sounded so clichéd, not to mention materialistic. "Why don't you tell me," I went on, trying to redirect the conversation, "what constitutes the Vietnamese Dream?"

Suddenly several hands went up, as if I was the teacher. The leader gestured to me, to give me the floor.

The first response, from Than Van, who would occasionally give me rides on her scooter: "You first attain a good job with a high salary. A stable job. You have a happy family—get married, nice children, good housewife. A lady's dream is simple. After marriage, she is assistant behind her husband. Her ambitions decrease; they stay in the shadow of her husband."

I could feel a frown forming on my face, and tried to hide it. Somehow we'd veered off into the topic of gender roles.

Another woman, Nien: "A good wife who makes money as a fabric seller at the market, and her husband not as much, she must secretly slip money in his trousers at night when he is sleeping."

Ms. Loan: "A woman's role is in the kitchen. She is a servant at home."

"Okay," I said. "Anyone else?" I was looking in particular at the men, who hadn't said a word.

A young man in plaid trousers with slicked-back hair: "You need a happy family. And a job suitable to me."

Then a young man everyone called "The Philosopher" chimed in. "Happiness is fleeting. If we can be in our heads and bodies at once—if you are *here*, can *hear* me—then you can be happy. It's just a theory."

I had no idea what he was talking about. Everyone laughed nervously. I glanced at the leader as if to say: please take over. Ultimately it was agreed, after some clunky discussion, that the Vietnamese valued family more than Americans did. Part of me wanted to argue, but the other part of me knew, in its own way, it was true. How many of them would not live near their families by choice; not live *with* their families by choice; or travel clear across the world, by choice, and thus not see their family members for many, many months, if not years? Americans did all of these things. I did all of these things.

"Our guest, Annie," the leader said suddenly. "It is her Mother's Day in America. Do you have any news to share?" I froze for a second, completely caught off guard by the nonsequitor. Any news about what? Lily had pooped twice in the toilet. We were soon heading off on a trip to Taiwan. My friend Tim back in Minnesota had died. But that was clearly not what he meant.

"Well," I said. "I was wondering if Vietnam celebrates Mother's Day as well?"

Everyone shook their heads and laughed. Mark and I always made a big deal out of holidays, and this year I'd received a beautiful necklace, a small statue, and a striped Hello Kitty tote bag from the kids.

I had spent so many Mother's Days away from my own mother that I'd taken to sending her earrings from afar. Over the years I'd sent her hummingbirds, silver hearts, dragonflies, Celtic knots, and once, when I'd been living in Idaho, some beautiful turquoise ovals.

This year, Mark and I had decided that for Mother's Day we would offer to buy my mother a plane ticket to Vietnam to come and stay with us for a couple of weeks. We would pay for everything once she got here, I assured her. "And we'll even give you the kids' air-conditioned bedroom all for yourself." I knew the heat would do her in, but thought I might be able to lure her anyway.

After a couple weeks, she finally admitted that her health problems were just too much and there was no way she could do it. "I'd love to see you and the kids, Annie," she wrote in an email, "but I'm not up to it right now. I can barely leave my own house."

According to Amy, my mother had been in pain and seeing doctors almost constantly since we'd been gone, all the result of her botched bladder surgery. Complications ranged from extreme abdominal pain to heavy bleeding to dizziness to headaches. Plus, Minnesota to Vietnam wasn't exactly an easy trip, and I knew it was crazy to expect her to get on a plane and fly clear across the world.

Without any transition or closure, the leader stood up and abruptly informed us we would now go across the street for *mang cau*, or apple custard shakes. I noticed that gradually the women had taken over the group and we'd lost many of the men, which I found ironic, given what I'd just heard about the subservient role of women in Vietnam.

When I got home later that day, Mark and the kids were just getting back. We were exhausted from the heat, humidity, and miscommunication, so we all headed up to our air-conditioned bedroom for "underwear naps"—my favorite thing in the world, an activity that involved going fully under the covers in just your underwear in the middle of the day.

When we woke up, a monsoon rainstorm had blown in and made everything even hotter and muggier. Mark and I sat in the living room drinking wine out of coffee cups; the kids played with a deck of cards that kept getting blown away by the fan. Big fat raindrops slid off the awning outside and splashed onto the cement courtyard.

It was Mother's Day, and I felt a rush of memories: the warm tuna hotdish my mother had waiting in the oven when I returned from the Peace Corps; the matching flannel pajamas she'd made Mark and me for Christmas, with retro kitchen appliances dancing all over them; the way she scratched the back of her head with her fingertips when she was nervous; the sound of her humming along to Jim Croce while she washed the dishes.

As I watched Hudson and Lily play, my heart ached that she was missing so much of their young lives. The kids would be so different when we got back, and even then, who knew how long it would be before we made it out to Minnesota to see her again.

Later, too tired to go eat at our favorite noodle shop, Mark and the kids rustled up whatever they could find. My Mother's Day dinner consisted of French bread stuffed with avocado slices, *pomelo* sections dipped in salt, and tiny bottles of strawberry Yo-Most—a simple yet memorable feast.

Digging

After more digging through my mother's memorabilia, I discovered she'd had other boyfriends in high school, which, although not surprising, made me wonder why she never shared any of this with me. One person was mentioned several times: Chuck Hansen. The name was familiar, and when I looked at his senior photo, there was a strange moment of recall: I used to babysit for him and his wife in Arlington. At some point, he'd lived just a block away from my parents' house on Main Street, was married to someone else, and had a new baby, whom I rocked to sleep and tucked inside a soft blue afghan.

But I needed further information, and luckily, some of my mother's high school friends were on Facebook. One morning I wrote to my mother's old best friend, Joyce, a flight attendant who now lived in Arizona. I asked her what she knew about Chuck Hansen and my mother.

Joyce wrote back later that day. *OMG. . . that is so weird. . . about 'Chuck'. . . cuz I was just thinking about when she dated him and what her life would have been like if they'd married. . . He lives up in Brainerd now. . . I think."* She continued. *"He was the most handsome man in high school. . . every gal wanted him and your Mom was his favorite. . . for awhile. . . can't remember if she dumped him or vice versa!! But they made a good-looking couple!*

The fact that my mother had been his "favorite" seemed to indicate he was a player of sorts, at least to me. And truth be told, he was incredibly handsome. Straight white teeth, an elegant nose, soft brown eyes, a full head of hair swept back off his forehead. When I placed his senior photo next to my father's, I couldn't help but compare them. My father had a more angular face, finer bone structure, thinner lips, heavy eyeglasses—perhaps less classically handsome, though there was something about him that was undeniably appealing—a quiet reservoir of... strength? Reserve? Angst? But the more I studied the photo, the more I saw a brooding, gathering storm inside my father's eyes; he wasn't smiling at all, as opposed to Chuck's easy, lopsided grin. Judging from their photos, the world already looked easier to manage for Chuck than for my father, and when I placed my mother's senior photo next to both of theirs, I'll admit, she and Chuck made the more stunning couple.

Over lunch one day, I told Mark about my mother's old boyfriend. We sat on the patio eating salad grown in our garden. We drank mint iced tea, and I kept explaining to Mark how much different my mother's life would've been if she'd turned one way instead of the other, if she'd ended up with Chuck Hansen instead of my father.

"But Annie," Mark said. "I'm so glad she didn't marry him."

I looked at him sharply, but then realized what he meant: I wouldn't be here. We wouldn't be here. Hudson and Lily wouldn't be here.

I was eager to get back to the computer, though, to see if Joyce had responded to my further questions. Luckily, there was a message from her on Facebook. *Your Mom was able to 'get' any guy she put her eye on!!!! Honest! I'm surprised she never told you about 'the past loves'!!! Keep digging... I can only imagine what you'll find! Can't believe she still has all that stuff!*

I kept digging, of course, and eventually came across my mother's class reunion program from 1987. Each class member had an update on his or her life twenty-five years after graduating. I immediately leafed through to find Chuck Hansen, curious to see what he'd written. But he provided no narrative, just his address in Brainerd, and his family status: *Wife, Karen (Laabs) AGI '65. Children: Nick, 9, Casey, 6, Bergen, 3.*

He clearly must've started a family late, because by that time, my mother had children who were twenty-three, twenty-one, nineteen, and eleven. What had he been doing in all the in-between years?

Then I saw his education listed: *B.A. University of Minnesota (political science), 1973.*

Masters of International Management, American Graduate School of International Management, Glendale, Arizona, 1973.

I was impressed, curious, and even more conflicted about my mother letting him "get away." Political science. A master's degree! With her love of journalism, they would've been so well-suited.

I turned back a page to see what my mother had written for her update.

I'm still living in Arlington with husband Lowell. We will be celebrating our 25th (silver) anniversary on Oct. 26, 1988 (Boy does that make me feel old!). I'm working at two jobs right now. I work at Morreim's Pharmacy and also do housecleaning in the cities.

We have 4 children. Our oldest son, Jim, is 23. He is presently living in Plymouth and working in St. Louis Park. He plans to work one more year and then go to school in Ely, MN, in some type of forestry work.

Our oldest daughter, Anne, 21, graduated from Augsburg College in Mpls. She just left for the Philippines Islands, where she is serving as a Peace Corps volunteer. She will spend the next two years teaching English.

Next in line is Amy, 19. She just moved to Bloomington a couple weeks ago and will work for a while. She is still always quite the "social butterfly."

The baby of the family is Mike, who is now 11. He will be in sixth grade when school starts this fall. He loves baseball and all the things boys that age like.

The way my mother presented her life with such quiet stoicism, such plainspoken brief biographies, the way she wrote "husband Lowell" instead of "*my* husband Lowell," made my heart ache. There was so much unsaid, such skillful excision of her troubled marriage, their overdue bills, the way her body had broken down from scrubbing floors on her hands and knees, the way Mike had grown into a depressed, difficult teenager who needed more help than my parents could give.

At the back of the program, there was a 5x7 group photograph at the reunion, everyone decked out in 1980s teal, fuchsia, and polka dots. My mother was tucked somewhere in the middle, and she had the exact same look—a glancing off to the side with her lips pursed—that she'd had in the high school photo taken in 1963. In the row behind her, someone stood out. He wore a bright blue polo shirt with the collar upturned, white pants, and sunglasses tucked into the placket of his polo. He was deeply suntanned with a sexy five o'clock shadow, a full head of dark hair swept off to the side, and a bemused look on his face: it was Chuck Hansen, the political science major, the MBA, the one who got away. He was still quite clearly the best-looking guy in the class.

He stood so close to my mother that he could've reached down and touched her shoulder. He could've wrapped his arms around her from behind and held her close. Except she was looking away. Standing between two smiling frosty blondes—the Lampe twins—something seemed to distract her. Perhaps it was her younger self in a plaid skirt and cardigan sweater, smiling and waving—all the hope she had, vanishing from the frame.

Quilt Scraps

Leaving Vietnam was harder than I thought it would be. I'd miss the way every single person adored our children and seemed to think they could do no wrong. I would miss the first-class and amazingly inexpensive manicures and pedicures, the way the coconut leaves swayed outside our bedroom window in the morning, fresh pineapple on a stick, avocado shakes. I would miss wandering the fabric market, then stopping off for an iced coffee at the little stall across the street. I would miss the little girl who lived just down the lane who wore all of Lily's old clothes and whom we called "Baby." I would miss bright neon everywhere at night, cheap Hello Kitty paraphernalia, *pho* noodles for fifty cents. I would miss my English Club friends.

One of the last things I did before leaving the country was to order a handmade Vietnamese quilt for my mother. I'd found a nonprofit quilt shop in Saigon run by American and Vietnamese women; each quilt was hand-stitched by a group of rural Vietnamese women and, after expenses, all the profits went directly to them. I loved this idea, and I knew that my mother, an expert quilter, would love it, too.

As the kids tore around the air-conditioned shop, playing hide and seek, I looked carefully at all the quilt patterns and fabrics. It seemed of utmost importance to get my mother something truly special to make up for all the pain she'd been through these past couple years after her botched surgery.

Finally, I chose a soft green fabric with cream backing, as well as cream thread for contrast stitching. There were so many beautiful patterns to choose from, but I kept coming back to the traditional lotus pattern. Since the stitching was so intricate and detailed, I knew my mother would appreciate the work that the women put into it. A cluster of lotus flowers bloomed in the center, framed by a border of smaller lotus flowers. Just thinking about the look on my mother's face when she'd open the box and feel the soft, handmade quilt in her hand tickled me. Its estimated time of arrival was two months; I could hardly wait.

I also made one last browse through the Can Tho fabric market. Over time, I'd come to know many of the shopkeepers, and when I tried to communicate to them that I would be leaving Vietnam for good, they swatted me on the arm as if I'd done something wrong. One of my favorites, Trang, was asleep, as usual, within the stacks of fabric that served as a little bunk bed of sorts. I had purchased a lot of fabric from her because she had the biggest selection, but also because I loved the way she laughed at everything I said, as if I was just hilarious, despite the language barrier (I have no idea if she understood me at all). She always pressed a small piece of candy or some fruit into my hand when we said goodbye, so I wanted to give her a small token of my appreciation.

Some of the other ladies woke Trang up, and she popped right up, as if she'd been expecting me. I wanted to buy all of her silk fabric scraps for a quilt my mother was planning to make for Lily when we returned. I tried to explain this to Trang, but it was too complicated. Finally, after I had a bag of beautiful silk scraps, I body-languaged that I was leaving on an airplane, but Trang just laughed and slapped me on the arm. I told her how much I'd miss her, then handed her a bag of things I thought she might like: our rice cooker, a favorite linen dress of mine that had shrunk, all of Hudson and Lily's outgrown clothes (I knew that she had several children), and a card with 500,000

Vietnamese *dong* inside (equivalent to about twenty dollars). I gave her a quick hug, then quickly rode away on my bike, since I didn't want to be there when she opened the card.

My mother and I had been scheming a quilt for Lily ever since I'd sent her photos of the beautiful silk that could be had for pennies in Vietnam. Lily was the only one in our family who didn't yet have her own quilt, and my mother said that if I could gather enough silk pieces, she'd design her something special. As a result, I'd been stockpiling silk in lovely colors like champagne, emerald, orange, cream, royal blue, and Chinese red.

"I'll make her something nice. Something with a little Asian flair," my mother wrote in an email. "Now just hurry home, okay?"

Back in Brockport, our old Victorian house felt enormous and ornate when we walked in. The stained glass windows, the marble fireplace, the built-in bookshelves and leather chairs and paintings on the walls all seemed staged and extravagant. The other thing I noticed was how eerily quiet it was on our street. The traffic that did occasionally flow past was organized and sane. Cars politely stopped for pedestrians. People paid attention to the four-way stop signs, and even waved each other through. There was the pronounced absence of beeping. A veneer of calm permeated everything. It almost made my ears ring.

Lily wandered around, trying to get reacquainted with her new space. She couldn't seem to find her way around. We had to keep telling her where the bathroom was. "Is this my bedroom?" she asked, touching Hudson's door.

"No," I said, leaning against his doorway. "Yours is right here." I opened her door and looked at the big shaggy pine tree outside her window. It felt woodsy and northern back in Brockport. On her floor was a toy box overflowing with dress-up clothes, dolls, and games, but she wasn't interested in the least.

"Where's the pool?" she asked.

"Honey," I said. "We don't have a pool."

Mark had disappeared somewhere in the house, and I realized that that's what happened to us at home. Our house was so large that we all got lost in it and were sometimes hard to find.

Lily ran up and down the long upstairs hallway. "Mommy!" she yelled. "Mommy? Where are you?"

I called my mother as soon as I knew she'd be awake. I could picture her sitting in her living room with the cat on her lap, her coffee clutched against her chest, her short, thin hair a nest of tangles. She'd be staring off into the distance with big eyes, the television mumbling in the background.

She picked up on the first ring. "Oh my gosh! You're home!" she said. "How are you? How was it?"

How could you adequately describe six months of living in Vietnam and almost a month of traveling around Asia afterward? "So glad to be home!" I said. "And the kids. Well. They're in heaven."

My mother cleared her throat. She was always froggy in the mornings. "Are they up? Can I talk to them?"

"Let me see." They were both in the sunroom, digging through old books. I held out the phone, whispered "Grandma Barb," and gave Hudson a stern look when he shook his head. Lily also scoffed and turned away.

"Maybe later," I told her. "They're still kind of figuring things out."

We caught up on what we could—how my sister Amy was doing, how Grandpa Pader was doing in the nursing home, how her new quilting business was starting to pick up—but there was too much to cover in one phone call.

"Tell me again about your surgery. It's tomorrow, right?"

"Yeah," she said, but her voice sounded off. Amy had told me that her pain and bleeding had grown worse with every passing month, so she'd finally agreed to try one last surgery at one of the best hospitals in Minneapolis. No more small-town, rinky-dink hospitals for her. "I have to be there at five thirty a.m. The surgery's at six thirty." Something really didn't sound right in her voice, and then it hit me.

"Are you scared?" I asked. She'd been through all of this before, had ended up twice in the ICU, and I could understand if the very idea of going in for more scared her to death. She told me they were going to try, once and for all, to repair what had been a botched job the first (and second) time around.

"I'm a little nervous," my mother said.

I tried to reassure her as best I could that this was a whole new team of doctors; patients traveled from out of state just to receive their care. "This time will be different," I said. "And you'll finally feel good again and can finally get back to normal."

She hemmed and hawed a bit, seemingly full of doubt.

"Well, don't be scared," I said. "It'll be fine. And when it's all over and you're feeling better, I'll fly out with the kids and we'll have a great time." I, too, was nervous—it was going to be a complicated, exploratory surgery—but mostly I was relieved that she was going to a bigger, better hospital and had a whole team of first-rate surgeons at her disposal.

After we hung up, I thought about unpacking, but had no idea where or how to start. Part of me didn't know what to do next, not just with unpacking, but with my whole life. That was the one problem with travel, at least for me: after returning home, it often brought about a sense of loose ends. Now what? We would go and get our accumulated mail; we would go to Target and buy the kids new clothes and a blow-up swimming pool; we would go to Wegmans and stock up on all the things we couldn't get in Vietnam: Frosted Mini-Wheats, bacon, Pop-Tarts, chips and salsa, frozen pizza, Sam Adams beer. We would slowly, dutifully, work through the piles of laundry, but then what?

Maybe travel really was, as Paul Theroux wrote, "a cure for nothing."

Getting out of the house always cures what ails, so I grabbed the kids and took them for a walk along the Erie Canal. It was good to get out, to see boats docked along the waterfront, to see joggers and dog walkers and the old guy who always sat on the same bench drinking his Colt 45.

"So, kids," I said. They ran ahead of me to throw rocks in the water. "This sure doesn't look like the Mekong River, does it?"

"I think it does," Hudson said.

"No, it doesn't!" Lily said.

"Yes, it does!" Hudson fired back.

I thought of the big steaming stretch of the Mekong River in Can Tho, how women straddled small wooden boats, paddling with long skinny sticks, how at night, across the water, that red-and-blue neon sign glowed: KYDAM LATEX MATTRESSES.

I watched cars rumble across the canal bridge. The sun was shining, but it wasn't hot. For a second, everything felt extremely vivid: the bright blue Jeep passing in front of me; the grass, richly and magnificently green; the white scalloped clouds against the blue sky; the crisp white wings of the swans floating along beside us. When we crossed over the Main Street bridge, everything turned ordinary again: the drab brick post office; the gray paved street; the beat-up plastic lawn chairs in front of Seward's Ice Cream Shop.

Jet lag was making my ears ring and my head spin. I felt as if I might pass out. "Let's all go take a nap together," I suggested. "Just like in Vietnam."

Hudson looked at me, genuinely perplexed. "But we're not in Vietnam anymore," he said.

The scent of Buffalo wings came drifting out of Stoneyard Grill. In the window of Red Bird Tea Shoppe, floral teapot cozies were for sale, twenty-five dollars each.

"You're right," I said. "We aren't."

The next day, I tried to unpack, but it was too overwhelming: dirty clothes, soggy books, crusty sandals, wrinkled boarding passes. Plus, I was anxiously awaiting news about my mother's surgery that morning. I poured myself a cup of coffee and wandered around the backyard with the phone in my pocket. I knew my mother's surgery was scheduled for first thing in the morning, but it wasn't until midafternoon that Amy called.

"You need to fly out here right away," she said. "Something went really wrong. She still hasn't come out of surgery." My mind raced with questions, but I didn't quite know how to organize or ask them. As soon as I received the call, Mark rushed out to Verizon and got us both cell phones, and I was on a plane to Minnesota by early that evening. The kids, who waved sadly to me from the driveway as I left, looked completely bewildered and terrified. We had all just gotten home from Vietnam! Why was their mom leaving already, and in such a hurry?

As I sat on the plane, I replayed the conversation I'd had with Amy. "When the doctors opened her up," Amy had said, "they said it was like hamburger in there. Everything was such a mess they could hardly see anything." I tried to will the image away, but couldn't.

"And where are you off to?" my seatmate asked as we landed. He wore a crisp blue suit, and had a prickly buzz cut and a pink, angular face. "Business or pleasure?"

"Family visit," I managed to croak out. I popped out my cell phone and acted like I was busy with it just so he would stop.

It was then I realized I didn't even know my own cell phone number, much less Mark's.

I can't remember who picked me up, what time of day or night it was, how I managed to maneuver through airports, highways, elevators, and hospital corridors, but there, in the ICU waiting room, sat my two brothers, Mike and Jim, tan and buff from their construction jobs. My father wore blue jean cutoffs and a faded polo shirt and nursed his usual travel mug of coffee. Amy, blonde hair up in a ponytail, chewed nervously at her fingernails.

There were quick hugs, a few tears, nurses in and out, doctors being paged over the loudspeaker. Eventually, Amy led me to my mother's room, and once I found out she had her own dedicated twenty-four-hour nurse, once I witnessed the profusion of machines and the high level of care she was receiving, my hopes began to flag.

"Mom, it's Annie," I said. A tube was taped to her mouth. She was bloated, ungainly and yellow. When I touched her arm, it felt waxy and taut. "Can you believe I came all the way from Vietnam just to see you?" I forced a laugh. She was unresponsive; the ventilator slurped air in and out.

Amy stood behind me, chatting idly with the nurse, checking to make sure nothing had changed. It was clear I had already missed a great deal. I was still, for this brief moment, an innocent. I did note that no one moved with any urgency around her. Whatever had happened had been managed, for the time being.

"Mom," I said. "Hudson and Lily are so excited to see you!" I kissed her cheek, and tucked her hair behind her ear. "They can't wait to tell you all their stories about Vietnam." I told her about how long our flights had been, how Lily had had a breakdown at the airport in Tokyo when she threw herself down on the floor and wouldn't get up, how all the kids wanted to eat now that we were home was Pop-Tarts and frozen pizza. I told her I'd brought home a whole bag of silk scraps for Lily's quilt.

And then there was no more to say. She looked almost alien in her new skin. Her eyelids were puffed up like dumplings. She was in the middle of a blood transfusion. Somewhere in there, though, I could see her familiar "Mom" face—the carefully plucked eyebrows, the mole on her left temple, her long wispy eyelashes. Amy came and stood next to me and we held hands.

When it became clear that none of us were going anywhere, we set up camp in the ICU waiting room. Chairs folded down into beds; a constant pot of coffee was at the ready; nurses wheeled in fresh pillows and blankets. Other worried-looking families, just like ours, sat with torn-open bags of chips and bottles of pop and *People* magazines and different cell phone tones going off around the clock. Our family took the rear corner, and it was there that I began to piece together what had happened to my mother.

Apparently, the mood had been light just before she was wheeled into the operating room. At one point, Amy reported, our mother was convinced she was being taken into the wrong room. "Well, great," she had joked. "Next thing you know I'll come out with a boob job." And she'd laughed. "Or maybe I'll come out as 'Bob' instead of 'Barb.'"

My brother Mike would later admit that he'd had a very bad feeling about the surgery all along.

And so, Amy continued, our mother had gone in for surgery at about six in the morning. They waited hours, Amy said, which was not uncommon, but still. When morning turned into noon, and noon turned into afternoon, they began to suspect something had gone wrong.

"And sure enough," Amy said. "Just as I was about to go ask if anything was wrong, the surgeons came out, still wearing their scrubs and face masks." The doctors sat down with them and explained that when they'd opened her up, everything was so bloody and swollen there was almost no way to see anything. They'd tried for hours to weed through blood vessels and organs to find any errant mesh fragments from the prior bladder sling surgeries. They did finally manage to extract a few tiny pieces, but that's when the problem started: she began to hemorrhage. And once she began to hemorrhage, they knew they had to stop the surgery and close her up or she would die of blood loss. But because it had been an incomplete surgery, instead of stitching her back up, they were only able to close the wound temporarily with a compression patch.

As she spoke, Amy seemed oddly calm in a way I knew couldn't last. She was the youngest daughter, yet was forced to play the role of family spokesperson. My father and brothers sat nodding but not speaking. They were definitely not the family leaders in any situation, but remained on watch, guarded, as if, should they get too involved, this all might become real. My father got up repeatedly to refill his coffee.

Amy continued, looking at a little green notebook for information she'd written down from the doctor's report. "Okay, so after they closed the wound, they wheeled her into post-op," she said, still sounding so sure-footed that it had to be shock. "And that's where she started bleeding again. They couldn't stop it." She looked at me, and I knew, no matter how this all played out, things would never be the same. "And then, I guess, that's when she went into hemorrhagic shock."

In anticipation of all the questions Amy knew I'd have, she explained that, as the doctor had put it, "bleeding begets more bleeding," and since my mother's blood wouldn't clot, there was more bleeding, and pretty soon her blood pressure dropped and her oxygen level dropped and her organs were deprived of oxygen and blood flow.

Bleeding begets more bleeding? Since when had the medical lexicon become so Old Testament?

"Her doctor also said," Amy continued, "that she's 'as sick as she can be and still be with us.'"

I hadn't had much experience in hospitals, particularly not in critical care, but I knew that "as sick as she can be and still be with us" had to be a euphemism for something unspeakable. "Sick" was when you had the flu. Sick was food poisoning, bronchitis, mono. To describe her as being "sick" was surely meant to ease a family's mind—or at least to keep our hysterics down. Wasn't the doctor essentially saying my mother was hanging on by a thread and was on every form of life support possible and even then there were no promises she'd come through this alive?

That's how I read it.

There was, however, one small thing to be thankful for: I was back home in the United States and not halfway across the world in Vietnam while this was happening. Could it have been possible that just two days ago my only concern had been whether to swim laps in the pool or in the ocean? Could it have been possible that just two days ago I'd been buying silver jewelry, traipsing around a butterfly farm, eating curry noodles and getting a massage? I thought about all the time I'd spent in Vietnam, all those days and weeks and months I could've been spending time with my mother.

If I had known.

The Miniature Museum

One dark and dreary Sunday, missing my mother, I started digging through my file cabinet. I needed some physical evidence of her. I found a little bundle labeled "Mom" and grabbed it. The few remaining letters I had from her were crinkly and without envelopes since they'd been tucked hastily inside packages full of handmade treasures.

Dear Anne and Mark,   Dec. 3, 1999
Here are your Christmas stockings, as requested. I hope you like them. If they are creased from packing, just hold them over a steaming pot of water, don't press with an iron. Also, enclosed are some old linens. I'm sure you can find a use for most of them.

The snowman ball is one I painted from a class I took at the high school—the Angel I just thought was pretty. The cluster of snowmen & women is something I made last year. If it's too "cutesy" for you, send it back and I'll give it to Amy. I really did put a lot of time into it.

The little silver cup and silverware was given to you, Annie, from Grandma & Grandpa Griep for your baptism (dated your baptism day). I thought you might like to have them.

I'm home today, and want to get some sewing done—After I run this up to the post office, do bills, set Grandma's hair, etc. etc. etc. etc.

Hope you enjoy digging through the box. Will send biscuit quilt next.
Love to you both,
Mom

Some of the letters, written on spiral notebook paper, actually had swatches of fabric safety-pinned to them. Next to a red and blue calico strip, her handwriting: *This is only enough for 2 valances. You two will talk this over well I'm sure.* This was always her tease: that Mark and I overanalyzed everything.

She was always making something for us: kitchen curtains, flannel pajamas for the kids, a table runner for the dining room table (*thought it would look nice for your holiday party*), hand-knit slippers for the four of us. Her letters were like artifacts with bright fabrics, wool yarn and pencil sketches dangling off the pages.

Then, in a stack of crumpled papers, I found a card with an Indian teepee on the cover.

CIKSUYA CANNA SNA, CANTEMAWASTE YELO
"whenever I remember you my heart is happy"

Dear Annie,

I am writing to "thank you" for sharing your trip to Kansas City with me. You have a way that makes me feel special about myself, a trait that doesn't emerge very often. I'm a real person, my thoughts and wishes are as important as anyone else's. It feels good to feel good!

You are a truly wonderful daughter and friend, and I love you so very much.

Much love,
Mom

I'd had to convince her for months to fly from Minneapolis, by herself, and meet me in Kansas City, where I'd be attending a conference. I told her if she could just get there, I'd take care of everything else, including a room for us at the Hilton. But it wasn't always easy with her. My pace was about twenty times hers; I was a jaded traveler and didn't have patience for the boring guided trolley tours she loved. In stores or museums, she'd want to look at every single little item. No matter where we went, she made sure to let the clerk/waitress/bus driver know that she wasn't from there.

"Well, now, what is the tax here anyway? We don't have sales tax on clothing where I'm from," she'd say, then wait with a little smile on her face for someone to ask where she was from. And to my surprise, people often did. Even the hipster clerk in the vintage shop seemed to enjoy chatting with her. "You're from Minnesota? Cool!" Still, it made me groan a little inside every time she did it.

At the toy and miniature museum, however, we both hit our stride. We stood for hours in front of perfect little rooms with tiny china plates the size of nickels. "Don't you just love mini?" she said. "I could live in there. I really could." Though she filled her house with beautiful quilts and pretty wallpaper, the place had begun to fall apart with neglect. The north wall in their living room had buckled with age and split, sending bits of horsehair plaster crumbling to the floor. Upstairs, Jim's old bedroom had become a storage room, one section of the collapsed ceiling held up with a two-by-four. Her kitchen still had an ancient sink with separate hot and cold water taps. The wood floors in the dining room rolled like waves on a lake. I could certainly understand her desire to live inside a dream dollhouse. It was beautiful in there, perfect, and no harm could come to you. I, too, wanted to shrink myself sometimes and hide inside the carefully appointed tiny luxurious rooms.

Hours passed.

"Ooo," she said. "Let's buy postcards!" She purchased several and sat that night on the bed in our hotel room, her bare feet wiggling in contentment. She wrote out cards to my father, my sister Amy, my Grandma Griep, her sister Beth. A couple times she'd look up, thinking about what to write, and catch me watching her. "Oh you," she'd say, and pretend to toss her pen at me.

One night I offered to bring her to a jazz club; I told her I'd cover everything and not to worry. She fretted about what to wear, though. Over the years, she'd put on more and more weight, and had grown self-conscious about how she looked. She dug through her suitcase and pulled out a pair of jeans, a cardigan, and a blouse. I was at the door, my bag slung over my shoulder, waiting impatiently as she shuffled around the room.

"Well, now, don't rush me," she said. "I'm not the big fancypants traveler that you are."

"Mom," I said. "Hardly."

She was still in her zip-up robe and black slippers, because, she claimed, "you should never go barefoot in a hotel room because there's no telling who might've walked their germs all over the carpet." I was completely caught off guard by this. Her house was not exactly white-glove clean. Even though she worked as a house cleaner, she'd long ago lost energy for her own domestic chores, and little by little, her house had developed cobwebs and dust bunnies galore.

As she fussed around, ironing her jeans, I realized there was probably a lot about her that I didn't know. I'd spent my entire adult life living far away from her, and it made me wonder how much I might have missed. Something must've flickered over my face because she said, "What?"

"Nothing," I said. "I'm just happy."

We walked the three blocks to the jazz club, my mother clutching her purse tightly to her side for fear of someone stealing it. The unfamiliar streets were dimly lit and I wasn't quite sure where we were going. When a group of rowdy young men passed us, my mother scootched just a bit closer to me.

"So did I ever tell you what your dad said to me once when I bought a jazz CD?"

I shook my head.

"He said, 'You don't like jazz.'" There was no pity or anger in my mother's voice, but instead a spark of pride, like she'd finally proven him wrong. "As if he knows everything about me."

I snorted in agreement, and hoped I wasn't getting us lost.

"Your dad thinks he's the only one who knows anything. He can be real cocky sometimes."

I'd never thought of him that way before, but now that she said it, I realized it was true. He could be moody, moralistic, almost haughty, like when, despite being unemployed with a family of six, he'd refused a job as a custodian because it was "beneath him." Or had it been laziness? He seemed happiest (and most himself) when he wasn't employed and could hang around the house all day, drink coffee, read the paper, watch sports on TV, and—his all-time favorite activity—nap, though he claimed he never, ever slept.

When my mother and I found the jazz club, it was dark, smoky, and hazy inside. There was barely room to move, but I maneuvered our way to a small cocktail table in the back. My mother looked cute (no other word for it) with a new shorter haircut, tortoise-shell glasses, and a blue cardigan sweater over a gingham blouse. I'd never seen her like this—so in her element despite not being in her element.

A saxophonist crooned under a pink spotlight on stage. We ordered steaks au poivre and *pommes frites* and I convinced my mother to join me for a half-carafe of wine. She wasn't a drinker, though, and claimed that just a sip or two would get her tipsy. When I poured us both a second glass, my mother seemed conflicted, her forehead creased with worry.

Being out at a jazz club in Kansas City with my mother felt surprisingly natural. It made me spin ahead to other fun trips we might take together someday. I finally made enough money to "sponsor" her, although I knew it shamed her to let me. "I have my own money!" she said during the entire trip when I reached to pay cab fare, the dinner bill, museum admission. But I didn't care. My mother had gone with so little for so long. And selfishly, I got my mother all to myself for three solid days, which was worth more to me than any amount of money.

Back at the hotel, I took off my uncomfortable boots and fought the urge to check my email. My mother instantly slid on her slippers, changed into her nightgown and robe, and grabbed a tote bag full of knitting. She sat on her bed, turned on David Letterman, and began to click her needles together in a quick and even rhythm.

"I'll keep the volume down," she said, glancing over at me. "I know you hate TV."

"I don't hate TV," I said. "Why do you think I hate TV?" I flopped on my bed still fully clothed and made up, as if I had somewhere to go.

My mother rolled her eyes. "Every time you come over, you always say how much it depresses you to watch *Martha Stewart* and *Ellen* and *Price is Right*."

"But it's just *daytime* TV that gets to me," I said. "Especially TV in the morning. I don't know."

"O-kay," my mother said, smirking.

"What?"

"Nothing," she said. She was knitting an intricate blue baby sweater for someone's granddaughter in Arlington.

"This is so nice," my mother said. "Isn't it nice? Just us like this." I noticed her feet rub back and forth in contentment.

"It is," I said. I closed my eyes and listened to the knitting needles click back and forth—a familiar, lulling sound. But before long the clicking stopped, and when I opened my eyes, I saw that my mother had fallen asleep, her knitting laid across her chest like a tiny blanket.

Rainbow

A couple months after my mother dies, Mark buys me a set of solar-powered dragonfly lights on black plastic stakes. I stick them in the yard on either side of the front porch entrance. I think they look elegant and sweet.

By day, I barely notice them—gray and translucent, they blend into the background. But by night, they glow purple, blue, green, red, orange, and yellow. I spend quiet nights sitting on the porch drinking wine while they slowly pulse every color of the rainbow.

Hudson is starting first grade, so every morning while we wait for his school bus, he and Lily, three, kick the soccer ball around our tiny front yard. Sometimes Mark joins in, too. Sometimes we all four play soccer at eight in the morning as if we have absolutely nowhere else to be.

We kick the ball hard.

One day, Lily accidentally hits one of the dragonfly lights with the ball and shatters its plastic wings off. Another time Mark kicks the ball so hard that one of the stakes breaks right in half, the dragonfly landing in the flower garden.

Where it doesn't glow anymore.

Camp Panning

It was a good thing Mark had booked me a one-way ticket to Minnesota, because, as the hours and then days passed, my mother's condition remained critical, and it became uncertain how long we might be there. My family and I spent hours together in the ICU waiting room. I learned how to use my cell phone and logged in everyone's phone numbers. For lack of anything else to do, I'd occasionally tell a story about Vietnam to fill the time.

"And then," I said, "when we tried to order our food, there was absolutely no English on the menu. So we tried to act out what we wanted, but when they brought us our food, there was a whole fish staring up at us with a big gluey eye, and then what looked like chunks of crocodile or lizard in a weird white gravy!" Or, "Once we were on a bus from Can Tho to Saigon and I was so sick Mark had to get the bus driver to stop. And so when we finally careened off the road, I stumbled out of the bus and into the hot pounding sunshine in the middle of nowhere, but then, suddenly, an old lady came trucking out of the rice paddies and caught me just before I fainted and made me lie on a little hammock under a tree and everyone on the bus got out and gathered around me like I was dying and then the old lady made me eat this weird brothy soup with little gummy rice balls floating in it and unbelievably it actually made me feel better but then..."

My family would chuckle, but there was no energy in it. We were all so tired that it was hard to keep up with the confusing stream of harried specialists and nurses who were forever on "shift change" and couldn't be bothered with our questions. The first few nights, as our mother precariously hung on, we never left the waiting room. We'd wait for someone to give us updates, but we quickly learned they never came unless we hounded someone. Afraid of missing something important, we ate all of our meals in the waiting room, taking turns running down to the McDonald's with our orders; we received visitors in the waiting room as if it were our own house; we watched TV in the waiting room, read magazines there, charged our cell phones there and generally treated it as our own personal living room.

When it got dark, we all settled down in the fold-out chairs and tried to sleep. Loudspeakers went off with urgent calls for doctors; the elevator dinged open and closed; fluorescent lights from the hallway blared into our eyes. Occasionally, other families would be there, holding vigil for a loved one. Lots of tears were shed; cell phones rang throughout the night; random relatives arrived and received updates; and sometimes cries of agony and grief would wake us all up when someone didn't make it. After that, we'd all lie there wide-eyed and scared, knowing that we could be next. I became a fan of Tylenol PM and earplugs.

In the mornings, we fell into a routine: coffee, of course, then Amy and I would go clean ourselves up as best we could in the public bathroom, then we'd all settle into our corner of the ICU waiting room to watch the local news. Each day when I woke up, a sense of shock hit me in three waves. One: where am I? Oh God, the ICU waiting room at Abbott in Minneapolis. Two: is my mother still alive? Most often one of us had already gone in to check on her, and would report: "the same." Three: I hope my kids are okay. After spending every waking minute with them in Vietnam, I missed them terribly. Mark had told them only what they were able to process at the time—that my mother was very sick and I needed to be with her right now. The most hurtful thing was that Lily refused to talk to me on the phone. She'd utterly given up on me, and was punishing me for disappearing from her life.

Every hour or so, one of us would go sit with our mother. When the nurse told me my mother might still be able to hear, I began reading her a book—a dumb book, some religious story about a girl in a garden I'd found in the waiting room—but it felt good to have something to do and some way to connect with her. I sang "Puff the Magic Dragon" and "Dream a Little Dream" but sometimes my voice cracked and I couldn't keep it up, especially with the nurse sitting in the corner behind a big panel of buttons like an airplane pilot, pretending not to notice me.

As time passed, more and more relatives, friends, and neighbors began expressing their concerns about my mother. Our phones rang constantly. How was she doing? Had anything changed? What was the latest report from her doctors? Though it was wonderful to know so many people cared about her, Amy and I found it exhausting to have to repeat the same details over and over, so I decided to start a blog. Writing had always been the only way for me to make sense of my experiences, good or bad. If I could just put into words what seemed too confusing or horrible or overwhelming, maybe, just maybe, I could get a hold of it and lessen its impact. By writing it, I felt as if I was in control, however false that might've been. Also, with so much medical jargon being thrown at us every day, I hoped that writing it down might help us all understand what was happening to my mother.

In a small waiting room down the hall, I found an unoccupied computer, and sat down to begin www.quilterbarb.blogspot.com. But after I'd chosen a cute floral background and a purple banner,

I froze. What tone to take? How much to tell? And, was it in poor taste to write publicly about my mother's deteriorating health?

I forged on. There was nothing else to do and so many people loved her and wanted to know how she was doing. We simply couldn't keep up with the calls.

Tuesday, July 10, 2007

I have started this blog to keep everyone posted on my mom's condition. She is currently at Abott-Northwestern Hospital, recovering from a surgery she had on Friday, July 6th. As many of you know, there were major complications following the surgery, most resulting from severe post-operative bleeding, which led to very low blood pressure, which led to acute hemorragic shock. There have been a lot of up and down moments, and she has indeed survived a code blue arrest, and we are all feeling very lucky to still have her with us.

Today we had some somewhat good news. Her blood has been coagulating better; she has moved from five blood pressure medications to two. They've taken her off the paralytic medication that has paralyzed her voluntary muscles so that the respirator can function better. All of these are good small steps. The doctors are also hoping to try and reduce her sedation and see how her thinking might be and see if they can reduce her reliance on 100% oxygen. They have stressed to us that she is still in very serious critical condition and she is still receiving the highest level of critical care, but we are grateful for the small steps.

We will keep you posted as we get more news. Thank you for all the prayers and love. You all mean so much to her and to us.

I found writing the blog to be a great comfort. Sitting alone in a dim room in front of a softly humming computer was how I spent a good deal of my life. My fingers hit the keys with familiarity and speed. And even though writing the words "hemorrhagic shock" and "code blue arrest" was harsh and frightening, simply putting them down concretely lessened the blow.

As soon as people got word of the blog, comments came streaming in. Terry, a woman my mother had cleaned for who'd become a true friend; Dave, my college friend in San Francisco; Roger and Karen, my father's relatives in Green Isle; Joyce, my mother's childhood friend; Barb and John, Christine and Paul, Ruth and Jeremy, my friends back in Brockport who'd been thinking of me and my mother. I read and reread their comments, clinging to them like a life raft.

Back in the ICU waiting room, we continued to settle in for what looked like a long-term stay: pilled afghans, wrinkled pillows, People magazines, bags of chips that my father's hand loudly crept into in the middle of the night. There were moments of levity as the time dragged by, stupid laughs that got us through the fear and stress of every minute. One day a box of Harry Potter Jelly Bellys surfaced.

"Here," my brother Mike said. "Try Puke." We all sampled Dirt, Snot, Earthworm, and Booger and ranked them. I remember my brother Jim nearly gagged on Booger, his eyes watering. I found Earthworm to be the most repulsive, with its musty dirt flavor; Sardine was a close second. Sometimes we'd put two into our mouths at the same time to see what happened. "Ew!" Amy said. "Try Ear Wax with Vomit." She spit out a pile into her hands. "I can't do it. Oh my God. Gross."

Another day we spent hours taking cell phone pictures of each other going cross-eyed. I laughed so hard I almost wet my pants. "You guys! Don't make me laugh!" I yelled, crossing my legs. I ran for the bathroom. We continued with the cell phone photos, trying to outdo each other for who could look the stupidest. Mike had an expert way of hanging his tongue out slightly, drooping his eyelids and turning just one eye inward. He won easily.

Despite the circumstances, I found great pleasure in spending so much time with my family again. Even when I came home to visit, I rarely got to spend time with my brothers, who lived two hours north of Minneapolis and quite a distance from my parents and sister. They both worked in construction, were completely obsessed with duck, quail, pheasant, deer, and even wild boar hunting (the last in Texas, on their annual vacation), and lived fairly remote, quiet lives. They were the kind of guys who wore stocking caps indoors, had garages filled with tons of camo and waders and decoys, and usually ate dinner at nine or ten at night after several rounds of beers. We always had a great time together, despite how relentless they were about teasing me.

I loved Mike for his constant gags, like imitating a convenience store clerk who always said, "Have a goo' one," or the way he got himself so riled up about stupid things like bumper stickers on cars that said things like, "I'm Only Speeding Because I Have to Poop." He would harp and harp on it, in utter disbelief that someone would actually go out of their way and buy it, put it on their truck and drive around with it on. "I mean, seriously, who would do that?" he'd say. "Who would take the time out of their lives for something so fucking stupid?" Then he'd repeat the message over and over and over until none of us could stand it anymore.

Jim, the oldest, was the quietest and most reserved of us all. Over the years, he'd gone from working light industrial jobs to a rough stretch of unemployment and uncertainty about his future, until he'd gotten into construction work with Mike. Despite their age difference, they'd always been close. Both of them would say, "I'd take a bullet for him," whenever someone noted their obvious loyalty to each other. Jim seemed happiest, though, when we all kept things positive and didn't discuss our childhood and especially our absent, neglectful father. He'd get defensive and say things like, "Hey, Dad was a good shit," even though Jim was the one who'd probably been affected the most by our father's alcoholism and shoddy parenting. Both of my brothers had good, tender hearts and loved animals, little kids, and a good laugh. But they were terrible at keeping in touch, which used to hurt my feelings until I realized that was just the way they were—take it or leave it.

We had coined our part of the waiting room "Camp Panning" and laughed when we saw what a messy hovel we'd created: dirty duffel bags, grocery sacks spilling out half-empty Gatorades and cigarettes, Doritos ground into the carpet. "Only the Pannings can white trash even a hospital waiting room," my brother Mike said, then stepped out for a cigarette.

Throughout all of this, our father sat in the midst of, but was not a part of. He'd never been good at communicating his feelings, and now, with his wife lying just around the corner on full life support, he retreated into himself even further. He was the one, I suppose, most in denial, the one who simply could not see through to the end of this. Not that any of us really could, but any time I went in to see my mother and saw the ventilator pumping her chest up and down, saw her hands and feet flicker involuntarily, felt her puffed, waxy skin, part of me felt the reality of her odds, how far she already was from being fully alive. But we all moved through each day with some amount of hope because we had to. And now and then the doctors would give us tiny crumbs of information that provided us with optimism. They'd lowered the ventilator's oxygen level and she'd done some "practice" breathing on her own; the open wound they'd had to leave taped closed after surgery still showed no signs of infection.

In fact, on one particularly gloomy day, Dr. Parnham, her intensivist, came to see us in the waiting room because he had "unequivocably good news" about our mother. "Unequivocably" got our attention, and we all sat up, completely riveted. He was a small soft-spoken black man with a strong Caribbean accent. He folded his hands in front of him calmly before speaking further.

"Her lungs are much better," he said. "She's down from one hundred percent oxygen to forty percent. That's a major milestone." This was, of course, thrilling news for us, and we set about a flurry of phone calls to relatives and friends. Part of me began to believe she might actually make it.

We all gathered in our mother's room, rubbing her arms, brushing fingers through her hair, filling her in on the good news—though she was completely unresponsive. Still, we felt buoyed up enough to actually leave the hospital after hearing the news. This was a huge moment. We hadn't been out for days. After making sure all of her nurses had our cell phone numbers in case anything came up, we headed out into the bright July day, which was surprisingly just like any other day. Doctors strode past in white coats holding coffee cups. Cars arrived to pick up new mothers and babies. Kids zoomed by on skateboards. The grass was still green; the sky was still blue. I looked up at the hospital and tried to locate my mother's room, but couldn't.

Despite its status as one of the best heart hospitals in the country, Abbott-Northwestern was in a pretty dicey neighborhood, just north of Lake Street, a hotspot for pawn shops, gangs, prostitutes, and drive-by shootings. But you could see some gentrification. The old Sears building had been converted into the Global Market, an indoor assortment of funky shops, stalls, and restaurants. It was dimly lit and smelled like curry and incense. You could buy Guatemalan bags. Clocks from Denmark. Silk Chinese fans. Cones of incense and rosewood incense holders. A frilly white dress for the upcoming Little Miss Puerto Rico contest.

We all took off to find something to eat, and my father and I ended up at West Indies Soul Food, where we ordered curried chicken with rice and hot sauce. What a treat, after so many pizza deliveries, McDonald's meals, and chips. But being out in the world again felt precarious. I checked my cell phone, then checked it again, then again. As I ate, I felt not happiness over the delicious food, but sadness that my mother could not be here experiencing this with us.

The curried chicken sat like a rock in my stomach, and every sip of Coke made it even heavier. Neither of us really talked while we ate. We glanced at each other, then looked away. We didn't know how to experience the everyday world anymore.

Since we were all out of clean clothes and toiletries, our next stop was Dollar General across the street. Some questionable, furtive activity seemed to be taking place between a couple of parked cars; little kids rode their bikes around the cracked parking lot. A dirty white T-shirt had been tossed, soaking wet, to lie by the entrance. But we needed things. We needed clean underwear, so we loaded up on six-packs of Fruit of the Loom. We bought sweatshirts because of the icy air conditioning inside the hospital. We bought socks. My father wandered around the store, lost, so I filled his basket with a razor, a black T-shirt that hung down almost to his knees (which caused us hysterical laughter when he wore it later that day), some Pringles, and a bag of root beer barrels. I had always loved browsing in dollar stores, but this one was closing in on me and I had to get out.

"I'll be outside," I told everyone. Standing in the parking lot, my legs felt weighted with lead. I held a bag full of socks, underwear, deodorant, and Pringles, but it was irrelevant. It solved nothing. The sun continued to shine while my mother lay in the ICU two blocks away, unable to breathe on her own, unable to speak, unable to say, "Oh, Annie! When did you get here?"

Dragonfly Pie

Every year, my inventory of dragonfly items grows. For Christmas I receive a beautiful pie pan with dragonflies painted inside it from my sister-in-law Maggie. My mother's friend, Marcia, embroiders me a dragonfly bookmark. During a visit, my sister-in-law Jacqui comes home from a day of shopping with a green dragonfly pot holder for me.

From my friend Barb: a soft brown T-shirt with a blue dragonfly on it.

From my friend Christine: a silver dragonfly brooch, its wings set in amber from the mountains of New Hampshire.

From my friend Sarah: three stone dragonfly garden steppers that greet me every time I come home.

From Mark: a delicate sterling silver dragonfly necklace.

From Hudson: a small black and white dragonfly he painted in art class.

After a week passed with my mother on life support and no indication of any real progress, my hope began to falter. When I looked at the situation from an outsider's point of view, I saw this: a woman had suffered hemorrhagic shock after surgery, suffered damage to all her major organs, and was being kept alive by life support; she showed no signs of voluntary movement or cognitive awareness. This was indeed what we were facing. And yet, the doctors kept feeding us just enough information to provide optimism: her lungs were functioning better; she was no longer receiving any blood pressure medications; they were trying to wean her off the sedation with the hope that perhaps she might be strong enough to have the surgery to close her incision. Because of her heavy post-operative bleeding, the surgery had been incomplete, and posed a high risk of infection.

Plus, my mother had already suffered two code blues at the time. Amy had to explain to me that when we heard, "Dr. Blue, Room 4176. Dr. Blue, Room 4176," it was a life-and-death emergency, and any available doctors had to rush to that room immediately. I'd missed my mother's first code blue because I was still in New York. Amy reported to me later that it struck her in waves. "My first thought was, 'Oh no, that's so sad,'" she told me. "But then I realized Room 4176 was actually Mom's room, and then it hit me and I panicked and thought I was going to puke."

My mother's second code blue occurred one night when an almost party-like atmosphere filled the waiting room. My Uncle Bill and Aunt Cleone had brought a pasta salad and a cooler of drinks; Aunt Beth brought a handheld Yahtzee game that Amy and I kept fake fighting over; my cousin Sara and her husband Jerry brought an assortment of delicious spreads and dips along with pita bread points, and we all sat there sampling them, ranking them, and trying to guess at their ingredients. A cheery mood infused the wait as more people arrived, all of them bearing food. My Aunt Frannie and Uncle Tom had called ahead to get our orders for pasta meals at Olive Garden and arrived with warm, garlic-scented take-out boxes. My friend Dave had sent a huge bouquet of flowers, and they sat in the middle of the table, releasing their sweet scent and brightening the room.

But suddenly a young nurse came rushing into the room and asked for the Panning family. Our whole group swarmed her as she said, "You need to prepare yourselves. Things are not looking good."

My Aunt Kandi grabbed everyone's hands to form a prayer circle. "Someone call Pastor!" she yelled. My father's knees buckled and he almost fell into the industrial coffeemaker that had kept us all going for weeks. My brothers hung their heads silently and Amy's husband held her close. I longed for Mark. I stood stiffly with my hands clutched to my chest.

"I think it's time to say your goodbyes," the nurse said.

We all filed forward in a weeping, clustered line, and followed the nurse to my mother's room. But, surprisingly, within seconds, her vitals snapped back to life and the big ventilator machine made chugging noises again. I watched the bright green line on the heart monitor go from flatline to tall peaks. But how much more could her body endure? She no longer looked like herself. Her skin had a claylike feel and color; her eyelids were puffed and shiny; even her toes, the nails painted her signature pale peach, looked ghostly and lifeless.

Later that night, I shuffled to the bathroom, brushed my teeth, took my Tylenol PMs, and tucked myself into the foldout chair that had become my bed. I lay on my side and tucked my hands under my cheek, but sleep was impossible. A bright shaft of fluorescent light shone into my eyes. Amy had her back turned away from me, and when I reached over to tap her good night, she squeezed my hand. I could hear her sniffling. Mike and Jim had stepped out for cigarettes, and my father was sitting in a dark corner of the room eating a bag of cheese popcorn.

Unable to sleep, I wandered down to her room where I could hear the ventilator pump up and down. It was dim, quiet, and oddly peaceful in the room, and I stood next to her bed and held my mother's hand. It felt warm and thick, as though, if I squeezed too hard, I might leave a permanent indentation. Her head was tilted slightly to the left, the ventilator tube taped to her mouth.

I started to ramble. "Mom, this is scaring me. Please, I need you to get better. You know, Hudson and Lily are so cute now. Lily got all grown up when we were in Vietnam, and did I tell you Hudson learned how to ride a bike there? He gets huge kudos for that considering the streets where he learned were completely swarming with motorcycles and scooters and taxis and bicycles going every which way without any thought whatsoever to stop signs or pedestrians. It took him a while but he finally got it. And Lily...well, you know what a go-getter she is. She actually conned her teacher at the Vietnamese school they went to so that every day Ms. Vang would bring her next door to the pharmacy and buy her candy."

Sometimes my mother would move her head or hand slightly, and every time my heart fluttered; perhaps she knew I was there. Still, the nurses had warned us that most of her movements were involuntary and not to read too much into them. I fell asleep that night sitting next to my mother in a chair, breathing to the rhythm of the respirator.

The next morning, tired of the runaround we seemed to be getting, I was determined to get some answers. I'd seen families ushered into the conference room by teams of doctors, and I wanted the same. Finally, after stalking her doctors and nurses almost all day and waiting what seemed like forever for them to finish their rounds, a care conference was scheduled for late that afternoon.

We all sat around the table where a box of Kleenex sat prominently in the middle. I had my pen and notebook ready. We were all fixated on Dr. Parnham, her intensivist, who finally reported that all of my mother's major organs had been "injured" during the hemorrhagic shock.

Injured?

When none of us said anything, he continued. "Here is what we know. Her kidneys have failed, her heart has decreased function, her liver and spleen show damaged spots, her lungs are not working properly, and her brain function is at this point entirely unknown." He stopped, as if to let the words sink in.

After a moment of silence, he asked if we had any questions.

I looked around. Mike and Jim sat sniffling, hands in their laps, as did my father. Amy, for the moment, was quiet. "What's the next step?" I asked.

"We need to keep her BP stable," Dr. Parnham said. We all nodded as if we had any idea how they would do that. "We also need to start weaning her off the oxygen to see if she may begin to wake up."

Wake up, as if she were simply asleep.

Dr. Parnham looked at the other specialists in the room, who nodded in agreement. Then, he turned to us. "Surely you understand that she needs to wake up to get off the ventilator."

"What about her brain function?" I asked.

Dr. Parnham softened, though I did see him take a peek at his watch. "At this point, it is unknown. With so much trauma to the brain, her brain cells are suspended in stasis."

"But what about—how can you tell?" I asked. "I mean, what can you do to find out?"

"More testing," he said. "Time will tell."

Amy then began asking him about her kidneys (still not functioning), her incision (she wasn't strong enough to have the site closed yet), and her prognosis, long-term.

The last question seemed to get his attention. He sat up straight, folded his hands on the table and gave us all eye contact. "Your mother," he said, nodding at my siblings and me. "And Lowell, your wife." He nodded at my father, whose watch alarm kept beeping, as he couldn't find a way to turn it off. "She is as sick as she can be and still be with us. All of her major organs have been damaged by blood loss. As long as she stays this way, it can be the same. But it can't get worse. She is still critically ill."

This sounded to me like a deeply complicated philosophical puzzle. I had no idea what he meant, but just when I tried to ask for clarification, a code blue alert came over the loudspeaker. Dr. Parnham rose from his seat, promising us more details later. He and the other doctors rushed out of the room.

"Fuck," Mike said. I was twelve years older than him and could still sometimes see him as a toddler running around in a little corduroy overalls. He rubbed his head.

"Was that supposed to be some sort of riddle?" I asked.

"What do you mean?" Jim asked. The oldest of us, he was the most stoic, the most prone to silence and avoidance.

"Well, when he said, 'As long as she stays this way, it can be the same. But it can't get worse.'" I had written down the doctor's exact words and read it all back to them. "What the hell is that supposed to mean?"

"Let's not overanalyze everything, okay?" Amy said. "Let's just go. Let's get out of here." She turned to leave and we all followed as if we were her children.

The problem was, we had nowhere to go but the waiting room, which was beginning to feel like a prison, especially since Dr. Parnham told us we'd likely be in for a long wait. Fortunately, I was on summer break from my teaching, but I felt bad for the rest of my family, who were losing wages with each passing day. My father's employers at the kitchen-cabinet factory—not the most understanding or humane people to work for—were causing us all a lot of anxiety. They maintained a strict work attendance policy, and if you missed a shift (even if you were ill) or came in late, you were given a "ding." After three "dings," you were out. My father had already had two dings, and, since he made absolutely no effort to address the situation, Amy and I spent hours on the phone with them, trying to work out a reasonable solution so that my father didn't lose his healthcare coverage—that was our greatest concern.

That night, after Dr. Parnham's sobering report about our mother, none of us could sleep. At one point, we all rode the elevator down to the dark, abandoned lobby, then sat outside in the little patch of yard in front of the hospital. Cars honked and thunked heavy bass as they drove by. Crickets chirped; mosquitoes whispered around our legs, biting. We drank lukewarm Gatorade someone had brought us in bulk. We didn't talk. There was nothing to say.

The next morning, after thinking about what the doctor had said, the issue of my mother not having a Do Not Resuscitate on file started to weigh on me. She and my father had never worried about such things; they were both barely sixty years old. Now, it seemed like a huge oversight. My mother had suffered so much. How many Code Blues could she endure? And at what point was "saving" her doing more harm than good? And what was her prognosis anyway? No one had really spoken clearly about her odds of survival, her chances of recovering fully or even partially.

She'd been in the ICU for almost two weeks and was still receiving the highest level of care. We'd seen people nearly dead from heart attacks recover and walk out with their families while we lingered like squatters in the waiting room. Still, the Do Not Resuscitate issue seemed like something my father, as her husband, should've been handling. But my father, the epitome of passivity and indecision, did not seem likely to bring it up or face the issue unless forced. I decided to hold off.

At this point, my mother's kidneys were not functioning, and what had started as daily four-hour dialysis sessions were now necessary twenty-four hours a day. After several more CT scans, her brain function was still uncertain. "She's had so much trauma," the neurologist told us, "it's like her brain cells are floating in syrup. It's hard to say."

Syrup.

Then, on July 16, Amy's birthday, my mother opened her eyes for the first time. My father, a naturally loud talker, had gone in that morning to hold her hand, when suddenly her eyes popped open. He ran to get all of us, still lounging like teens with our cell phones on our fold-out beds.

The nurse on duty, however, tried to caution us. "I don't want to ruin your excitement or anything," she said. "But sometimes eye opening can be a purely physiological response." She gave us a warm smile and clutched her clipboard. "Just like when she moves her hands and legs sometimes. That's not voluntary. That's involuntary."

Still, how could we not be excited? Her pretty brown eyes! Plus, it seemed obvious that every time she heard Dad's loud booming voice, her eyes really did pop open. But after the initial excitement, we all noticed there wasn't much "there" in her eyes. There was only a blank, flat, faraway distance. Her pupils were pinpricks. She didn't fixate or focus on anything. I had to look away.

On the plus side, however, she did become well enough to have the surgery to close her incision. One of the surgeons warned us, though, that because her condition was still critical, surgery might prove more than her body could tolerate. As a precaution, they were bringing in massive amounts of blood should she hemorrhage again and need transfusions.

During her surgery, we sat in a basement waiting room, dark and dim as a bar. A big-screen monitor showed the status of each patient's surgery just like the flight monitors in airports.

"This is exactly where we were for Mom's first surgery here," Amy said. She chewed her fingernails.

"I don't know if I can take much more of this," Mike said. He was never good at sitting idle. "I'll just be over here." He pointed to a small, glassed-in TV lounge. "Come and get me as soon as you hear anything." I knew he was antsy for a cigarette, but none of us dared step away for even a minute.

Jim closed his eyes while sitting straight up and seemed to fall asleep except for every few seconds he sniffled and itched his nose.

I looked up at the monitor. PANNING, B. IN PROGRESS.

I picked up a magazine. Condé Nast Traveler. "No Shoes, No Shirt, No Worries: 29 Eateries on 11 Caribbean Islands." On the cover, a woman in a white bikini waded into the soft blue ocean. Seeing the beach catapulted me back to Vietnam, then to Thailand and Malaysia, which we'd visited on our way home. Just two weeks ago I'd been parasailing above Penang Bay, sailing under a rainbow parachute high above the ocean. Two weeks ago I'd hiked up Wat Arun in Bangkok with Lily on my back and lit a candle at the top for my mother. Two weeks ago I'd eaten fresh mangos for breakfast, napped with the kids in air-conditioned hotel rooms, and slowly started getting ready to return to our lives in New York. Would my kids ever forgive me for abandoning them so completely after six months of nonstop togetherness? I ached for them and their warm little bodies. Even though I talked to them at least twice a day, there was hurt and caution in their voices.

"When are you coming home?" Hudson would ask, but I couldn't give him a straight answer because I didn't know. Lily would talk to me for a few minutes, then start crying. "Mommy, I miss you!"

I checked the monitor. PANNING, B. IN PROGRESS.

I paged through the magazine, surprised to find a small mention of Vietnam in an article, "World's Best Street Food." In Saigon, they'd found a food cart that served banh mi, a sandwich with grilled pork, cucumber, pickled carrot and fresh cilantro inside a short crusty baguette. I'd grown to love banh mi when we lived there, but more than missing the food, the photograph of the busy, bustling street made me miss our lives there. We'd gone to Saigon almost every few weeks, and stayed at the Elios Hotel, where they knew us by name and always had treats and toys for Hudson and Lily. In fact, on Lily's third birthday, the hotel manager had come up to our room with the most elaborate birthday cake Lily would probably ever see in her life. I missed the chaos, the way that travel, if you let it, could change you—for the better.

I checked the monitor. PANNING, B. RECOVERY.

"Oh my God!" I said to Amy. "She's in recovery." We both called out to Mike and Jim, and before we knew it, the surgeon came out in green scrubs, smiling. He took a seat beside us in the waiting room. "Well, you'll be relieved to know it went very well," he said. His face mask dangled jauntily around his neck.

"No bleeding?" Amy asked.

"Nope. Her edema is down; her organs seem viable. We didn't have to use any skin grafts or implants. She did much better than I expected."

We thanked him over and over, and only then did it hit me how sure I was that she would die during this surgery. Now, without the threat hanging over us, the relief was palpable, stunning, a bit bewildering.

I convinced Amy to have a drink with me at Figlio, a bar and restaurant in Uptown that I used to frequent as a college student. We sat outside on Lake Street and nursed glasses of chardonnay that sweated in the late afternoon sun. We laughed and giggled and could not stop exclaiming over Mom's good luck. We went into Calhoun Square, where I bought white capris and a black T-shirt at Express. There was a fancy kitchen store that sold high-end impractical items and I bought a teeny tiny colander in cobalt blue, though I had no idea what I would ever do with it.

"That is so cute!" Amy said. "You're just like Mom. You both love mini."

"Totally," I said. "You know what? I'll give it to her for a little present when she gets better." But then I thought: *if* she gets better.

"Well, I suppose we should head out, huh?" I said.

"I suppose," Amy said.

We drove back to hospital quietly, two sisters, both of us mothers, without our mother.

One summer's day, while the kids were running through the sprinkler and Mark was at the gym, I came across one of my mother's scrapbooks in my study. It was brightly colored with leggy scissors and paintbrushes dancing on it with a twenty-nine-cent price sticker in the corner. The pages inside were yellowed and smelled of musty basement with a slight tang of violet perfume. I inhaled deeply.

Inside, neatly arranged and expertly glued into place, were all the trappings of the perfect life she must've imagined for herself. Every page contained ads for Early American and Colonial furniture. A wingback loveseat with "box kick pleats" in brown or cactus green for $129. A Frigidaire Cook Master Electric stove in "Mayfair Pink, Sunny Yellow, Turquoise, Aztec Copper, or Snowcrest White." A Gabberts canopy bed of solid maple for $89.95. The ad copy read:

SO PRETTY YOU'LL HATE TO TURN OUT THE LIGHTS!
No doubt about it! A canopy bed makes the loveliest bedroom for anyone.
And what girl (of any age) wouldn't love one all to herself? Use it with dainty canopy top or simply remove canopy to create a stately four-poster.
Nothing down—$5 month.

I was heartened to know that although my mother never got all the perfectly coordinated furniture she'd dreamed of, at least she'd gotten the canopy bed. As a child, I used to love lying in my parent's canopy bed, pretending I was riding in a fancy carriage. Sometimes Amy and I would hang lightweight blankets over the canopy sides to create a fort; the light spilled in hazy and mottled and we'd spend hours in there with our Barbies. It was perhaps the only good (read: new) piece of furniture they had.

As the years went by and money was tight, my mother set her sights on smaller, more inexpensive things that she'd stockpile away in boxes upstairs. She always thought she was going to make big money off these things that she'd purchased for a dollar or less.

"These paper dolls are going to make you kids rich someday," she'd say, smirking when we teased her about what a hoarder she'd become. An old kitten-shaped teapot that she'd given to me years ago constantly came up in conversations. "I hope you remember what that's worth and don't ever get rid of that," she'd say to me. "That's going to be worth a fortune someday, Annie."

My sister and I would roll our eyes.

"You two!" she'd say. "You better listen to your mom on this one." She'd shake her finger at us.

The scrapbook with all the artfully furnished home interiors had been left unfinished. In fact, after the first nine or ten pages, it was empty. It struck me now how soon the tapering off of the furniture ads must've began, how quickly the dreaming must've subsided. How long did it take, I wondered, for my father's alcoholism to end up costing them everything? They'd married in October of 1963: how long was it before she realized she'd never get that Mayfair Pink electric oven? November? December? How long before she knew it was best not to keep compiling ads for a lovely life she would never inhabit?

If I could have my mother back for just a day, I would ask her these questions and beg her to answer them. Please tell me, I'd ask her over a cup of coffee on her front porch. *Why did you marry him? You were so smart and pretty and talented! You must've had some idea what you were getting into. Didn't you? Did you really love him that much?*

As I leafed through the mostly empty pages, I found a smattering of magazine clippings in the very back. An afterthought? A later burst of hope? There was a small article pasted among them: "5 Good Tips on Using Color in Your Home." These weren't ads, but fully realized (and highly idealized) photographs of elegantly groomed women showing off their emerald and coral bedroom linens in pristine, well-lit rooms. One photograph struck me with its simplicity: a beautiful open staircase with holly wrapped around the banister and a small table festooned with Christmas gifts. It looked almost exactly like the front staircase in my own living room, right down to the holly and the Christmas gifts.

The final clipping was a country-blue kitchen with a maple table and chairs, set perfectly with orange and yellow napkins, placemats, and plates. The yellow checked curtains coordinated with the dinnerware, as did the seat cushions. The table overlooked a large picture window with a view of a sprawling yard and an oak tree. I liked to imagine my family sitting around that table, me as a kid swinging my feet back and forth; Amy, Jim, and Mike asking politely for more mashed potatoes and gravy; my father in a shirt and tie slicing into his steak with a fork and knife. Buzzing around the table in all her domestic glory would be my mother, filling our glasses with milk, asking if everything was all right before carefully removing her floral apron, folding it over the back of her chair, then settling down in her pink shirtwaist dress and pearls as she served herself a modest portion of green peas, then beamed at her gorgeous and well-kept family.

Instead, my mother served frozen pizza for dinner, which we ate right off the box, two small ones for six people. We lived in the trailer court at the edge of town, and our backyard was the town cemetery, which became our playground. We'd run wild while our parents were at work and ride the gravestones like rocking horses. In winter, you could hear ice and snow tick against the trailer's metal exterior, and more than once, during summer tornado warnings, my mother would rush us down toward the cemetery to hide behind those same gravestones for safety, since we had no basement. The things I always dreamed of and wished for that we never had in the long skinny trailer: windowsills, or a telephone. The telephone we simply couldn't afford, and instead of real windowsills, nice deep wooden ones on which I could set Precious Moments statues, or spider plants, or stacks of books, we had little strips of metal around crank-open windows. The house was, after all, meant to be mobile, a fact my mother hated but which she tried desperately not to say out loud.

While my mother lingered on life support, days trickled by with no clear prognosis. One doctor told us she might need a tracheotomy, since it's not good for a body to be on a ventilator for more than two weeks. When I asked him how long she might need to be ventilated, he hedged. His eyes, behind thick glasses, flicked back and forth like a lizard's. "Well," he said. "That's unknown." He cleared his throat. "But you may want to make some long-terms plans for your family."

No one seemed to know anything for certain. I desperately wanted to grab one of the nurses, doctors, or specialists by the shoulders, shake them (gently) and say, "Please just tell me what you think. Give it to me straight! Is my mother going to make it? Based on what must be thousands of horrible cases you've experienced, how does my mother's compare? Do we have any reason whatsoever to hold out hope?"

We decided we couldn't all stay here every day, week after week, so we sat down and drew up a schedule. After much discussion, it was decided that because I'd just gotten back from Vietnam and hadn't seen my kids or Mark for so long, I would fly home for the rest of the week, and Dad would stay at the hospital. "The boys," as we referred to my adult brothers, would go back to Ironton and work the rest of the week. Amy would also go home, go to work, then drive up in the evenings to be with Dad. I would fly back the following week, at which point we might know more, and reassess.

I found it hard to leave, though. What if she suffered another code blue and I was somewhere in the air over Michigan? What if she came to and I wasn't there? What if—? I stood beside my mother's bed and held her hand, which twitched occasionally. I told her that I had to leave, but just for a while. "I'll be back before you know it," I whispered. "And I'll take all kinds of pictures of Hudson and Lily so you can see how much they've grown."

The late afternoon sun, so buttery and rich in Minnesota, poured through the windows onto the foot of her bed. I kissed her hand. "I love you so much. Get better, okay?" My hands shook as I walked away.

The tiny plane to Buffalo was exactly the kind of cocoon I needed to be tucked inside. I got the last evening flight. When the lights dimmed, I ordered a bottle of red wine and fell asleep instantly.

I cried at the sight of the kids waving to me in the airport. Lily's hair was already so much longer, and though Mark had tried, her little ponytails were tangled and loose. Hudson didn't crack a smile. I held their soft little bodies, then fell into Mark's big, solid chest.

Back home, I picked absently through my giant stack of mail. Though it was a hot and humid July night, I snuggled the kids close to me, inhaling their scent. Lily asked me to read her four books instead of one, which I did. Hudson wanted me to linger after I tucked him in.

"What's wrong with your mom?" he asked.

She had a surgery and had a lot of bleeding so they're trying to make her better.

"How long will she be in the hospital?"

They don't really know.

"Do you have to go back there?"

Yes, but not for a while.

"When do you have to go back?"

Not until next week.

"Can I come with you?"

Oh, Sweetie. I don't know about that. She's very sick and kids aren't really allowed in the hospital.

"Have you seen my new Lego set? It's got a real elevator thing in it."

No, really? Show it to me!

Mark grilled us steaks and zucchini for dinner and we drank white wine on the patio. We talked idly about the kids, house projects that needed to be done, our friends' latest travels, but not much about my mother. I slept harder that night than I'd slept in weeks, and barely heard the phone ringing downstairs early the next morning—too early for most people to call.

It was Amy.

By late that afternoon I was back on a plane.

Oh, kids, I thought. *Please forgive me for leaving you again.*

When I joined my family back in the ICU waiting room, there was a new sense of urgency and fear. There was now bleeding in my mother's lower intestinal tract. A colonoscopy had revealed a perforated colon that would require emergency surgery to repair—only she wasn't strong enough, the doctors explained, to survive a surgery.

That was when everything went blurry.

Phone calls were made. Relatives gathered. At some point, I remember asking for a social worker to help us navigate the next phase. There was still the matter of my mother not having a DNR on file to contend with. If none was put into place, the doctors explained to us, they were legally obligated to keep resuscitating her.

Sooner than I expected, a social worker was brought into the conference room to speak with us. Her name was Marcia, and her gray pixie cut, her eyeglasses on a chain, her brown batik tunic, comforted me.

"I know you probably feel lost and scared and confused," she said. "And that's perfectly normal." She had also arranged for one of my mother's doctors to come in and give us the latest report. Dr. Finney sat at the other end of the table, smiling wanly, exhaustion deep in her eyes—but still she tried to radiate energy and concern in her face, and in her tapping pen.

"Please just tell us everything," I said. "We want to know exactly what it is we're facing here."

My brother Jim coughed and sniffled. I had my pen and paper at the ready.

Dr. Finney began. She explained that my mother had sustained very serious damage to her colon. "It doesn't appear that her bowel has recovered from the blood loss," she said. "In most cases, we would immediately remove the colon, but in your mother's case, she would have very little chance of surviving an operation of this magnitude at this time."

Amy reached for a Kleenex. None of us spoke. I heard Mike sniffle.

"So little healing has occurred," Dr. Finney went on, "that it's almost impossible for her to survive this." She looked at us all levelly. "In fact, at this point, I'd say the probability of survival is less than five percent."

My father's watch alarm went off, beeping frantically, and he did nothing.

"Dad," I said, reaching over for his wrist. "Please turn that thing off." But he didn't know how to and neither did I.

Mike shifted in his seat. "So, like, if she did happen to survive despite those odds, what would be, you know, the situation?"

Dr. Finney nodded, as if Mike had asked exactly the right thing. "Well, if she would survive this," she said, "and that's a very big if, chances are she'd be on twenty-four-hour dialysis, maybe forever, and she'd be on a ventilator with a trach, maybe forever, which would mean she'd need to be in a long-term care center."

"So, what," Mike said, "like a nursing home?"

Dr. Finney winced a little. "No, nursing homes aren't equipped to handle ventilator patients. It would have to be a long-term critical-care center."

Did the doctor mean my mother would be on full life support in some high-tech care center for the rest of her life? Would she ever wake up? Would she talk? Eat? Walk? "What about her brain function?" I asked. "That seems like the last piece of the puzzle that we keep waiting for."

Dr. Finney nodded again. I noticed she wore diamond stud earrings and a matching necklace in white gold. Her lipstick was deep magenta. "Her brain function is still unknown," she said, re-crossing her legs, "although by this point, after reducing her sedation meds several times, we'd hoped for some kind of response by now."

During this whole discussion, the social worker, Marcia, kept taking notes on a clipboard and occasionally peeking at her cell phone. She wore Birkenstocks with light blue polish on her toes. "So if I can just interject," she said. "What we're here to do now is ask some important questions. Namely, if your mother, your wife, were sitting here around this table and heard what's just been said, what would she want? Knowing the odds, the damage that's been done and the poor odds of survival, what would be her wishes for resuscitation if she were sitting right here?"

I could see her strategy, and had to admit it was effective. Imagining my mother hearing all of this horrible news made me certain she would in no way want to be kept artificially alive. I glanced around the table, but all I could see was everyone's red, crying eyes.

Marcia went on. "If her heart should stop again, what would she want? And then you need to ask yourselves, 'If her heart does not stop and continues on like this indefinitely, what would she want?'"

I felt the answer was clear, but I couldn't read the rest of my family.

Marcia leaned over toward my father and offered him a Kleenex. His nose was dripping and he was letting it. "Lowell, as Barb's husband, what are your thoughts?"

"Well," he said. He wore his usual polo shirt tucked into jean shorts. My aunt Frannie had gone to Target one day and bought him a whole bagful of new clothes. He'd modeled them in the waiting room one night for everyone, getting some good laughs. "Well, I think we need to talk to our pastor," he said. "And then maybe we can figure out what to do."

Marcia and Dr. Finney both nodded sympathetically. They were probably pleased this was going so well. We weren't throwing fits; we weren't demanding second opinions or screaming or tearing out our hair or wailing in agony. We were an obedient, low-key bunch.

"Well, not to pressure you," Dr. Finney said. She slid her chair away from the table, indicating we were almost done. "But I would make sure, given her precarious state, that you sort it out sooner rather than later," she said. "If she keeps bleeding like she is and her heart stops again, I don't know how much more her body can take to try and bring her back."

A horrible image of my mother's damaged body being pumped, prodded, and jounced around like a rag doll haunted me. *Just put a DNR on her file right now!* I wanted to shout. *Please! How much more can we let her suffer? How much more can she possibly take?* But I was not her husband, and I was only one of four children, so we needed to treat this decision with as much care as possible.

My father, siblings, and I all went down to the first-floor chapel, where we sat on the floor in a circle. I remember thinking that we should all hold hands, but we didn't. A warm yellow light glowed behind a large cross on the wall, though there were also nods to other religions: a Buddha statue, a Native American painting, the star of David, a copy of the Quran.

I was trying very hard not to push anyone, but the idea that at any minute my mother might go into cardiac arrest, that the doctors would be called upon to resuscitate her despite her body's weak condition, panicked me. How could we do that to her? But this was a life-and-death decision. This was not something to be rushed. And I don't think that my father, unlike all of us kids, had ever entertained the possibility that my mother might actually die. It was his M.O.—to turn the other way, to ignore problems and hope they'd go away, to let someone else (usually my mother) figure things out. Now here he was, head of the family, father of four, trying to do what did not come naturally to him: make a decision.

I ached for him. Though he did not always treat her kindly or with much respect, he loved her deeply: my mother was his everything, the center of his universe. Without her, groceries would not be bought, meals would not be cooked, clothes would not get washed, friends and relatives would not be called, bills would not be paid, birthday cards would not get sent. It was hard to imagine what would become of him without my mother.

"Can someone see if Pastor is here yet?" my father asked. "I need to pray with him and ask for help." One of my brothers either made a phone call or went up to the ICU; I can't remember how it went, but I do remember the feeling of time ticking precariously as we waited.

Apparently Pastor Hanneman couldn't be reached, so one of the hospital's in-house "spiritual staff" was summoned. When he walked in, though, I almost laughed. He was so young. Slight in structure and short with red curly hair and freckles, he exuded about as much authority and reverence as a twelve-year-old boy. He was Howdy Doody, Tom Sawyer, Opie from *The Andy Griffith Show*. So clearly nervous, he clutched his Bible, raised his eyebrows at us, and asked, "And so who is Lowell? I'm Pastor Becker. Actually, I'm a pastor-in-training, but, you know, I'm here for you."

Classic Panning luck to get the completely awkward pastor-in-training at the most pivotally important time in our lives. But my father responded well to him, put him at ease, even though it should've been the other way around. I'd often seen my father shine in these instances. He always took the young guys from AA under his wing, or the guys at work from Cambodia and Vietnam, or random people he barely knew in our hometown. It was something I used to feel jealous of: how come he would be so warm, personable, and affectionate with people he knew only peripherally, when he would barely say a word to me and didn't show the slightest interest in what I was doing in my life?

The young pastor held my father's hand and indicated we should all bow our heads in prayer. When it was done, my father expressed his concern about whether he would be doing the right thing or not by signing a DNR.

At this, the young pastor rose to the occasion, and I'll always be grateful to him for that. "Well, Lowell," he said. "It seems as if God has already made the decision about Barb. And now all he needs is for you to accept it. What's happened to Barb physically cannot be undone. For whatever reason, this is the path God has chosen for her. In a way, there is no decision to make, because God has done that for you."

His logic seemed skewed to me, but the important thing was that it gave my father permission to do what he must've known, deep down, had to be done. It allowed him to "decide" without actually having to decide.

After chanting the Lord's Prayer with us, the pastor left us alone. My head pounded from plugged-up snot, stress, crying, lack of sleep, and the growing realization that I was likely going to lose my mother.

We left the chapel and rode the elevator up to the fourth floor, our floor. And, as luck would have it, we ran into one of my mother's doctors in the hallway. I didn't mean to, but I blurted out that we'd made a decision to do the DNR. Dr. Parnham nodded his head slowly. Then, instead of sitting us down in the conference room and going over official paperwork, he simply shook my father's hand. "An act of mercy," he said. "You are a good man."

It was done.

A strange calm settled around us after the decision was made. We gathered in my mother's room, the urgency gone. My heart beat quietly in my chest. I wanted it to end, but I never wanted it to end. I was so tired that I could barely think, but then I began to understand that I didn't need to think. I needed to be present, physically and emotionally. There was no need for analysis at this point.

The nurse treated us with a new tenderness. "I'm going to take her off the machines slowly," she said. "It'll take a while to remove the vent tube. But afterward I always give families the option of keeping her on partial oxygen. It's up to you."

"What would that do?" I asked, confused.

She said something about prolonging life, but we all agreed that my mother's pain had been prolonged too much already. We declined.

After the breathing tube was removed, the IVs pulled, the room grew so quiet it was eerie. All these weeks, the hum of the machines had created a sense of purpose, the chugging sound of hope that perhaps recovery might be within reach. Without the noise, without the busyness and distraction, my mother seemed sicker than ever. She did breathe on her own, though, which gave us all a little flutter of hope. Maybe the doctors had been wrong! Maybe they had no idea what they were talking about!

"It could be minutes," the nurse said. "It could be hours. Sometimes it can even be days." She took a small plastic container, opened it, and rubbed something onto my mother's lips that looked like watery toothpaste.

"What's that for?" I asked.

"Oh, it's so her lips don't get parched and dried out." With a tissue, she rubbed away some extra that had smeared on my mother's face, and for a second, I had a glimpse of what it would be like with my mother in a long-term critical-care facility.

The lip balm smelled like coconut.

When the nurse clipped a tiny white square of cloth above my mother's bed, the strong soothing scent of peppermint filled the room. I quickly figured it out: to mask the smell of death.

Time ticked by. I stared at my mother's lovely face, fully visible now without the ventilator and tubes. Her perfectly arched eyebrows, her high cheekbones, her thin soft hair—I wanted to memorize every detail.

Sad to learn is the hard fact that when you see an adult dragonfly it is in its final stage of life, and that final stage is only about a three-week period.

—Mike Gannon, a.k.a. The Pond Hunter

Which is exactly how long my mom fights for her life in the ICU.

Down in the Valley

The doctors decided, since my mother was no longer in need of urgent care, to move her to the oncology unit. We would only understand later this was where they brought patients to die.

Still, leaving the ICU was difficult. We'd become fast friends with so many families that it hurt to leave them. Just the day prior, an Indian woman with a three-year-old daughter had suddenly lost her husband. It was around lunchtime, the sun shining bright and clear through the plate glass windows. We'd known her husband had just turned forty and had a history of heart problems, but was otherwise strong and vibrant. I heard her scream from down the hall, and a few minutes later she came out to tell us she'd lost him. "I've been robbed!" she cried. "I've been robbed in broad daylight!" Her parents tried to shield her small daughter from the outburst, but it was impossible. The girl was tiny, dressed in a fancy pink sari, with very large eyes that blinked rapidly in confusion.

Later, we spoke again by her husband's bedside. She'd wanted our whole family, near strangers, to come and see her husband before they took him away. "He was such a handsome man," she said. "Such a good father." She ran her fingers through his hair. It didn't seem strange to me, her desire for us to see his body, to witness the site of his death. Perhaps no one would ever quite understand her loss as we all did—that exact moment, frozen in time, when the heart stops, while sunlight continues to pour through the windows, nurses continue to joke with each other at the desk down the hall, air conditioning continues to flow through the vents.

Then there were those who did make it. One woman with two teenaged sons had come in after her husband had a massive heart attack while mowing the lawn. We'd been spending lots of time with her in the waiting room, exchanging stories of what had happened and why we were there.

"It was the funniest thing," she said. She was tan and wore gold jewelry and white jeans. "The paramedics arrived almost immediately and submerged his entire body in ice. They completely *froze* him! I guess it's some new procedure that only Abbott is doing—the first in the whole country to try this."

Her two teenaged boys sat flipping through wrinkled *People* magazines, but I could tell by their darting eyes they were taking in every word.

The woman went on to explain that the procedure increased the chances of a patient's survival, and also a patient's ability to avoid brain damage by as much as fifty percent. Soon she reported that he was sitting up, then talking, then eating. He was almost fully recovered, even though his heart had stopped beating for over three minutes.

One day she came in smiling with a box of doughnuts for us. "We're actually going home today," she said. We hugged her and cried with happiness for all of them; no one in the ICU waiting room ever begrudged anyone their good news. We knew how random it all was, how it could just as easily have gone the other way.

"Good luck with your mom," the woman said. "We'll be praying for her every minute." And then they were gone.

My mother's new room in the oncology unit was tiny. We settled in quietly, almost reverentially. One of my mother's old high school friends had delivered a full-course Italian meal, complete with plates, cutlery, glasses, even a small jar of Parmesan cheese. We tried to eat it.

A new nurse with a pierced nose and burgundy highlights, much younger and hipper than any we'd encountered in the ICU, tried to prepare us for what to expect. "Now that the machines have been turned off," she said, "she'll stop breathing on her own time." She went on to tell us some signs to watch for that would indicate death was near: longer periods of pausing between breaths, dramatic changes in breathing pattern, breathing through wide-open mouth, extremities cool to the touch, bluish or purple coloring in feet and hands.

Knowing the signs, however, didn't prevent full-on panic from striking us when one of them occurred. Whenever her breathing slowed, or when she sometimes made a gasping noise, we all jumped to our feet and gathered over her, only to have her fall back into her old breathing pattern again.

It slowly grew dark. My mother's other close relatives came to say their goodbyes, and though we tried to give them privacy, sharing goodbyes and tears with them seemed inevitable and necessary. In fact, watching my Uncle Bill hold her hand and tell her it was okay to go, that we all wanted her suffering to end, nearly broke my heart. He'd lost his wife, Sandy, my mother's sister, to cancer; he understood the importance of this moment. His daughter, my cousin Sara, also came. Something about their presence, though, also brought me strength and peace. Their tears, their courage to say goodbye properly and bravely in the face of such sadness, made me realize how deeply my mother was loved, what a wonderful web of connection she had to family and friends.

When it had grown completely dark, the nurse brought us blankets, pillows, and extra chairs, and told us about a sleeping room down the hall with comfortable recliners. We were all exhausted, but reluctant to leave the room since we had no idea how long we really had with our mother. But the room was cramped with little room for seating, so we decided to rotate in pairs of two, the boys taking the sleeping room first, Amy taking the small waiting room just down the hall, and my father and me on first shift right beside her bed. If anything at all changed, we promised to send one of us *immediately* to get the others.

Later that night, I leaned my head against my mother's chest, singing "Down in the Valley" to her over and over. I'm not sure why I chose that song. There was something so peaceful about it: "Hang your head over / hear the wind blow..." It was hard to keep a steady voice; tears often stopped me, at which point I'd lean my body over my mother's and try to feel as much of her, physically, as possible. "Mom," I whispered into her ear, "thank you for your love and kindness. You have given me so much."

I kissed her soft, thin hair. My neck hurt. It was hard to hold the position. Plus, in the dark, I could hear my father sniffling.

We dozed on and off. Occasionally, a nurse would come in to monitor progress. She wouldn't say anything but would very carefully and quietly close the door.

Eventually, our exhaustion must've won out because I woke up, confused, and found Jim, Mike, and Amy in the room. It was apparently second shift, but I didn't want to leave. None of us did. We stood in the dim room, circled around our mother's bed, and held hands. My head was pounding, though, so I left to see if I could find some Tylenol.

The oncology unit was so much quieter and more subdued than the frenzied, high-tech chaos of the ICU. There were floral curtains, quilted wall hangings, fleece blankets folded over couches that didn't feel or look institutional. This was no longer life and death; it was death—looming, whispering, waiting—and the hospital staff wanted to make the journey to the other side as comfortable as possible.

For a moment, I sat in the small waiting room facing the big-screen TV. It wasn't turned on. I wrapped a blanket around myself, closed my eyes, and sat there quietly.

"Hey!" I looked up to see Jim poke his head down the hall. I took off running, nearly losing a flip-flop as I rounded the corner.

"So, I don't know what happened," Jim said. "I think she stopped breathing. I mean, I don't know. I'm pretty sure."

The room glowed pale blue like an aquarium. The air was hot and stuffy, stale with the scent of sweat and menthol. My first reaction was: Get the nurse! But my next reaction was: No. Let us all simply be here and fully experience these last moments with our mother.

I smoothed the purple log cabin baby quilt that still lay across her body; it had been with her the whole time in the ICU, a random bit of home someone had grabbed from her house to cozy up her sterile high-tech room. Later, much later, it would become the baby quilt for Mike and Maggie's first child, Wesley. I held my mother's hand, which was puffy, waxy, and already growing cool. How could this be over already, I wondered, when just a minute ago she was alive? When just hours ago we were all standing around with wilted paper plates of lasagna, the sun setting spectacularly outside the window in the buttery, orangey way I'd only ever seen in Minnesota? When just yesterday we were in our old wing of the ICU, drinking coffee, chasing down nurses and doctors for information, hoping against reason she might still make it?

Even when you're expecting death, you don't expect it. All these weeks as she'd lain unconscious, part of me knew I was never going to talk to my mother again, hang out in her kitchen while she made us fried-egg sandwiches, go antiquing with her to all the little junk shops we loved near Arlington, hug her hard when one of us had good news or bad news or just felt lonely and lost. Because I wasn't religious in any traditional sense, I didn't believe that prayers would, or could, reverse the physical damage her body had suffered. I was a hardcore realist, a "give me the worst-case scenario so I can prepare myself" person, but how do you prepare to say goodbye to your mother, especially when she wasn't even able to speak or hear you? Still, as I stood beside her, holding hands with my siblings, that's what we did: goodbye, we said.

I heard my father let out a low whimper like a wounded animal. Instead of looking at our mother, he kept staring at the floor, running his hands through his hair. During all these long days and weeks, he'd never cried hard the way we all had. He'd leak tears, then suck them in. Now, his whole body was shaking in a way that scared me. Mike approached our mother, told her he loved her, then had to walk away. Amy cried so hard I thought she might hyperventilate. Jim stood holding onto the end of the bed.

"Take all the time you need," the nurse said, then left us alone. I hadn't heard her come in, and realized she must've been keeping an eye on us the whole time.

We stood around my mother's body. She was done struggling, and for that I was grateful. But my heart quivered to imagine what lay ahead: a whole wide-open life without her. She would not watch my children lose teeth, play saxophone, graduate from high school, go to college, get married. She would not make her famous frosted Christmas cookies again, or knit us boodle slippers or sit on her front porch embroidering dish towels or say, "Oh, hi Annie! I was just thinking about you," when I called.

We held hands silently. There was so much love in that room; I knew I would never feel that much love all at once ever again.

Eventually, though, we knew we had to leave. It was almost three in the morning, and there were so many things to do. Finally, after much discussion, Jim and Mike left for Ironton; they seemed far, far away in mind and body as they said goodbye, and I worried about Mike behind the wheel. But they would need funeral clothes, would need to check on their dogs before coming back the next day. After they left, Amy, my father, and I sat together next to my mother. I'd never had much experience with death up close, but I didn't find it eerie. I found it calm. This was my mother. This *had been* my mother.

When we finally decided to leave, I found I couldn't. "We can't just leave her here all alone," I said.

"But Anne," Amy said. "It's not really her anymore. She's gone." My sister had lost a best friend in my mother, someone she ran to Target with at the spur of the moment or sat on the porch drinking iced tea with or regularly invited to her daughters' dance recitals and soccer games. I ached for her loss as much as my own.

After my father had brought all our belongings to the car, it was time to leave. We walked down the hallway, but I came back one last time to look at my mother's body. I stood in the doorway, but Amy was right: it was no longer my mother. Finally, I released my hand from the door frame and walked away.

Lemon Dessert

One day, during a recent summer, I got a craving for my mother's famous lemon dessert. Over the years, Amy and I had often called each other up in search of the recipe. "Is this it?" Amy would say, then read off a list of ingredients. "No," I'd say. "That sounds too much like lemon bars. It doesn't seem like it would have that light, whipped texture like Mom's did."

I remembered my mother making the dessert on the nights she hosted Sewing Club, an informal group of friends who got together once a month and worked on various sewing projects while they visited, drank coffee and ate dessert. The location rotated month to month, and likely my mother dreaded her turn, because we lived in the trailer court—I knew this brought great shame to her.

The women all had names like Pixie, Diane, Faye, and Jeannie. This was the 1970s, and although I have no recollection of feminism hitting our small town, my mother and her friends did exemplify a certain female solidarity. The sewing part of the club was just an excuse for them to gather. As Amy said later, "It was almost like an ahead-of-their-time book club." Men were entirely absent. My father probably loved it because it gave him a free pass to go to the bar and drink. I loved it because I knew it meant lemon dessert was on the menu.

I'd looked and looked through my mother's recipe box, which was white with strawberries around the lid and very sticky. One day I brought it up to my study and accidentally dropped it, ruining years of careful organization and order. As I sat there trying to sort the recipes into the correct categories, I noticed that some of them were in my mother's handwriting and some of them were in my grandmother's handwriting. I began to wonder: had my mother also inherited her mother's recipe box, just as I had inherited hers? Like her, I would now add my own recipes to it, making it a three-generation collection of family recipes. My grandmother's era (Bacon Grease Molasses Cookies), my mother's generation (Tater Tot Hotdish), and my generation (Chicken and Chickpea Tagine). The difference between my recipes and theirs, though, besides the profusion of ethnic dishes, was that theirs always provided a careful crediting of the original sources: *Tuna Hot Dish (Aunt Rosemary)*, *Egg Casserole (Church)*, *German Sugar Cookies (from Alma Meyer via Laura Litfin)*. Mine, on the other hand, were absent personal links, a hodgepodge of cultures, places and influences I couldn't credit even if I tried.

I searched through every single recipe but couldn't find the lemon dessert. I did, however, find an odd recipe:

HOT DISH FOR 50

2 lbs.	egg noodles, boiled
2 lbs.	Velveeta cheese
3 lge. cans	tomato soup
8 lbs.	hamburger
½ lbs.	onions, chopped
1 stk.	margarine

For *fifty*? I wondered. My only guess was that my grandma had gotten it from church. Maybe someone from the Ladies Aid had given it to her, since whenever a member of the congregation died, each "lady" was required to bring a large hotdish "to pass."

I also found the recipe for my grandma's spaghetti sauce,

once my favorite. I hadn't thought of it for decades, and seeing it triggered an intense memory of pleasure and comfort. It was the mildest, gentlest spaghetti sauce ever. She'd sauté minced onions in butter until they were very, very soft, then add a can of Campbell's tomato soup, a spoonful of sour cream, and a pinch of sugar, then simmer until it bubbled. It made her tiny kitchen, adorned with the huge painting of the Lord's Supper, steam up and smell sweet and tangy.

But still no recipe for the elusive lemon dessert.

For almost a week, I left messages for Amy, asking if she had the recipe. Finally, one day in July, she called me back. After catching up on every little thing, I circled back to the lemon dessert recipe.

"No," Amy said. "I never found it, but I think I have it in my head. It's called Borden's Lemon Dessert."

"What? You've had it in your head all this time and never told me?"

"Well, no. I mean, it's hard to explain. I remember parts of it."

"So let's hear it!" I said. "I have a pen. I'm ready."

It was a gorgeous summer day. Sun spilled onto my desk and all over the recipe cards I'd dug out of my mother's box. I scribbled everything down while Amy narrated the recipe to me.

"So you take one package of graham crackers, just crackers, no butter or anything, and crush them all up for the crust. It's weird how pans can be so different. It should be enough if you use a regular pan."

I asked her if she used the one our mother had given her for a birthday, the same pan she'd given to me—an aluminum 9x13 with a sliding green cover engraved with "AMY."

"No, mine got a hole in the side of it. Wore out. Anyway—oh! Save some of the cracker crumbs to sprinkle on top. Okay. Then mix two cans of Borden's or whatever brand sweetened condensed milk. Then the juice of four real lemons. I tried it once in a hurry with fake lemon juice and it was terrible. But maybe use five lemons. I can't remember. Just taste it a lot. It should be tart."

"Okay," I said, writing it all down.

"So then," she continued, "refrigerate that for a while. Then whip like a big carton of real whipping cream, and add sugar—just enough to make it nice and sweet but not too sweet. Then sprinkle the extra graham cracker crumbs on top. And it's best overnight. To chill it overnight. You know, so the wet stuff kind of soaks into the crust. Yeah, umm. I think that's it."

I told her how excited I was to make it, which brought up a whole other conversation about our mother, and Sewing Club, and the past.

"You know what today is, right?" she said.

"I know," I said. July 27 would always undo me. "It seems like it was just yesterday she was here."

"Really?" Amy said. "It seems so far away to me. Like it was so long ago."

I could feel the way time had softened the edges of my memories. I could still see my mother's warm brown eyes, but the basic shape of her face was slipping from me, the way she held a cup of coffee or chuckled as she was telling a story—fading, bit by bit.

"Anyway, I should go," Amy said. "I have to go shoot T-ball pictures today. It seems like that's what I've been doing all summer long."

"Yeah," I said. "I have to go get the kids."

After we said goodbye, I found one of my mother's blank recipe cards, and began filling it out.

"Mom's Sewing Club Lemon Dessert," I titled it. And then,

giving credit where credit was due, I wrote, "From Barb Panning, via Amy Panning Hardel, July 27, 2011." I tucked it back in the sticky recipe box in the section labeled "Sweets," and felt a small piece of history settle into place.

My mother's funeral was not at all what I'd hoped for, and to this day I feel ripped off. When my family met with the pastor of my parents' conservative Lutheran church, I immediately felt a wall go up. When I told him that my mother loved the song "Amazing Grace," and that we'd like that played at her funeral, he began flipping through the hymnal, grimacing.

"Well," he said, as if I'd just suggested that we blast the B-52s throughout the church and dance naked down the aisles. "That hymn doesn't really go with the Bible verses I've picked out. I was thinking of this hymn here." He pointed something out, but I didn't even look.

I glanced at my siblings to see if they were as irked as I was, but their eyes seemed to plead with me: *Please* don't make a scene. *Please* don't cause a fuss. Please just go along with things. But it was our mother's funeral! Didn't anybody care? Wasn't anyone willing to fight? Some jerk-off pastor was trying to suggest we couldn't even play my mother's favorite hymn at her own funeral?

I waited, but no one spoke up. Reluctantly, not wanting to upset my siblings, I let it go.

After the pastor hijacked any sense of personal significance from my mother's funeral, we met next with the funeral director, Shawn. We had all agreed that my mother's body would be cremated. But what to do about burying her ashes? Shawn pulled a three-ring binder off a shelf and opened it to a page of urns ranging from gaudy decorative gold to cheap plasticky green. Even though things had gone poorly with the pastor, I was determined to make at least some part of the funeral reflect who my mother truly was. "Well," I said, "I don't think we really want any of those." Not only were they ugly and generic, but they were expensive. I just couldn't see paying for something we didn't even like and that our mother certainly would not have cared for.

I looked carefully at my siblings to see if I was speaking out of turn. It seemed that whenever I came back to Minnesota, I was always riding an edge: the deep desire to fit in and be a good sister, a nice aunt, an agreeable person who gets along well with everyone, alongside the equally strong desire to make things happen, take initiative, and break through the thick, indecisive limbo we so often fell into like quicksand. But this time Amy nodded at me encouragingly, and I could see from the look in her eyes that she wasn't happy with the urns either. I shrugged my shoulders. "Maybe we could use one of Mom's antique metal picnic baskets." I cleared my throat nervously. "I think she'd like that."

My mother was an avid collector of many things, including Moderntone dishes, miniature tea sets, and vintage paper dolls, but her most recent obsession was antique metal picnic baskets that she kept stacked in the corner of her dining room. I loved their brightly colored patterns and designs. I loved their sturdy wooden handles. I loved that she kept them stashed full of embroidered dish towels, old linens from Ireland (from her sister, Sandy), newspaper clippings, random photographs, and old letters—most of them from me.

The poor funeral director—he could probably see his profits fading fast—collected himself, sat back, then said, "Sure, sure. Why, that sounds just fine." He then mentioned that a hole would have to be dug for the burial, and that they provided that service—for $300.

Again, I just couldn't see paying that much for something so simple, and after gathering support from my siblings, said that we would prefer to do it ourselves.

Again, Shawn wavered, and pressed his hand to his forehead. He looked exactly like what he was: an ex-high school jock, right down to the balding buzz cut, the hulking slouch, the jiggling, restless leg under the table. "Well, that's highly unusual," he said. "But, ah, I suppose it can be done."

My two brothers piped in that it would be no problem.

"The hole is required to be five feet deep by five feet wide," Shawn said. "Even for burying ashes. Those are state regulations."

Again, my brothers said no problem. They both worked in construction and said that digging a hole would be easy. Some small joke was cracked about their muscle power or something and everyone laughed uncomfortably for a second. Then, I second-guessed myself. Was I bargain hunting for my own mother's funeral? Was I? Yes, in that my parents had no money; they never had and never would. I knew my father would have no way to pay for anything, and even though all of us kids had been helping out financially, there was a limit to how much we could do. But no, as well, in that I wasn't really trying to save money. I simply wanted my mother's funeral to be as artistic and homespun and wonderful as my mother was. And I must admit I thought digging the hole ourselves would be good for us, would be a tangible act of finality, would add a concrete physical aspect to a death that still seemed so unreal.

Digging the hole for my mother's ashes, though, was far more difficult than any of us had imagined. First of all, it was hotter than hell. There wasn't a tree in sight and no shade whatsoever in the entire cemetery. Second, it hadn't rained for weeks, and the grass was parched, dry and brown. Third, we'd had to scrounge through my father's garage, where we found mostly old, junk shovels that had lost their sharp edges. Finally, after calling around, someone produced a hole digger for us, but the ground was so hard-packed and dry that it barely made a scratch. We dug and dug, taking turns, instantly getting blisters on our hands. Amy's husband, Dan, came to help, and he, along with Mike and Jim, ended up doing all the work while Amy and I stood there watching.

Mike popped his head out of the hole and threw a pile of dirt toward me. "So here's to another great idea of Anne's," he said. He was almost completely underground except for his head sticking out of the hole. Sweat covered his face; dirt stuck to the sweat; his T-shirt was soaked and smeared with brown.

"I know, I know!" I said. "I really know how to put a funeral together, don't I?"

No one said anything. There was still another whole foot left to dig. I looked over at the low-income apartments across the street. Behind them were fields of sweet corn, just about ready for picking. It was a late Saturday afternoon and utterly quiet. It struck me then that coming home to Arlington would never be the same without my mother there to rush out onto the porch and greet me with a great big hug.

"But wouldn't Mom have loved this?" I said. "Wouldn't she have loved us all out here, doing this together?"

Jim stepped away for a smoke. "I'm not real sure she would've," he said.

"Still," Mike said from the hole. "Three hundred bucks. That's effin' ridiculous."

My parents had never even had a savings account, and after all those weeks of missed work and lost wages, after all the massive hospital bills, my father was going to have a tough time financially. They'd always lived paycheck to paycheck, always promising creditors that next month they'd send a little more. My mother said she hated to answer the phone most days because more often than not it was a bill collector, threatening her if she didn't make payments immediately.

The hole finally dug, we drove back down Main Street to our parents' house. There, we looked through our mother's metal picnic basket collection for just the right "urn." We finally settled on a retro kitchen design: a dancing teakettle, an ear of corn, a fork and spoon, a slice of watermelon. It was charming and sweet, not something you'd associate with death. We loaded the packet of my mother's ashes into it (exactly the size and shape of a five-pound bag of sugar) and carried it out to the car.

Mark flew in later that day, bringing with him all of my requested items: the brown wrap dress I'd bought in Singapore just weeks ago (never imagining I'd be wearing it to my mother's funeral), my brown heels with the tortoiseshell buckles, my matching silver necklace and earrings, my camera, my pink slip, my favorite hair spray in the black bottle. The kids stayed with Mark's brother and sister-in-law in New York, going ahead with a long-anticipated camping trip. At the time, it seemed like the right thing to do, but later I regretted the decision. Afterward, whenever I spoke about my mother, Lily didn't really know who she was in any specific sense. My mother had only seen Lily two times—once when she was three months old, and once when the kids and I flew to Minnesota when Lily was not yet two. For the rest of Lily's life, she would remember her grandmother only through what I passed on to her as inherited memories.

After my experience with the pastor, I dreaded the funeral, of course, and true to form, the church service was terrible. Instead of personalizing it any way or telling stories about my mother, the pastor simply recounted all the spiritual "milestones" of her "life in Christ": her baptism, her confirmation, her marriage, her "dutiful" faith as a member of the congregation: blah, blah, blah. The service was so generic it could've been about anyone.

But wait! I wanted to shout. *What about her amazing generosity? And her mischievous smile? What about the beautiful quilt she made me when I got married that collects all the homemade clothing scraps of my childhood in one beautiful piece I will treasure for the rest of my life? Did you know it was hand-stitched? And what about that time when we were up at Grieps' cabin and some goats came running out of nowhere toward us and she was so scared she locked herself in the car and wouldn't let me in and I had to climb onto the hood and we both laughed so hard we wet our pants? And what about that sweet creamy banana milkshake she made me right after I'd had the surgery to remove those pre-cancerous cells? And what about that first prom dress she sewed for me—peach gauzy floral with satin ribbons that she tied at my shoulders with warm hands? What about the way I made her laugh once by pretending to be a crazy person and circling bright red lipstick all around my mouth while she doubled over in helpless laughter? And what about her goodness, knitting handmade slippers every Christmas for nursing home residents she didn't even know?*

What about that? I wanted to shout at the pastor. But instead I sang the hymns he'd chosen. I listened to the Bible verses. I closed my eyes. I held my sister's hand.

Patient's Belongings

One of the things I got after my mother died was the bag from Abbott-Northwestern Hospital of her "Patient Belongings." It was a standard-issue plastic bag with a drawstring at the top. When I first grabbed it from my parents' house after the funeral, I could see it contained the clothes she'd been wearing the day she went in for surgery in July, as well as other personal effects. Although some people might think it seemed morbid, having these things was important to me, since I hadn't been there with her that day as they wheeled her into the operating room. The bag of her clothes was one last link I had to her, one last tangible contact I could hold in my hands.

It took me quite a while to gather the strength I needed to open that bag. For months it sat in a corner of my study, and for months I kept telling myself I wasn't ready. I went back and forth in my mind about it. They were just clothes and objects. What did they matter? But they were so much more than that. For me, having always lived a great distance from my mother, these were not just objects but *were her*. I wanted to rip the bag open and be done with it, but at the same time I wanted to hold off forever, since it would mean letting go.

One day Mark decided to take the kids shopping at the mall. Hudson and Lily had both grown so quickly that all their pants had become high-waters almost overnight. Lily was only six, but often people would ask, "What, she must be eight, nine?" Our pediatrician had told us that, according to the growth charts, Lily was in the ninety-seventh percentile for height, and would likely be almost six feet tall as an adult. Hudson was much the same, and had, in his nine-year-old way, grown finicky about what he wore. To my disappointment, he'd come to favor mesh athletic wear in colors like royal blue and gold. I favored a classic blue-jeans-and-T-shirt look for him, but in order to avoid a scene, we decided Mark would take them to Old Navy this time.

It was fall and cooling off a little more every day. I'd shifted from drinking my favorite chilled herbal waters in flavors like Lavender Mint and Ginger Lemon Peel to sipping mugs of Earl Grey Tea with cream and sugar. I padded around the house in my favorite Levi's, a University of Montana sweatshirt, and cable-knit slippers. Martha trotted along beside me, no matter where I went in the house. When I sat at my computer, she'd curl up right beneath my feet. When I went to get the mail, her little nails clicked along behind me on the hardwood floors.

There were numerous things I should've been doing, primarily grading papers, but when I went to get my book bag, tossed on the floor in haste, my foot came in contact with the hospital bag. Chalk it up to procrastination, curiosity, or timing, but I grabbed it, finally, and opened it.

I laid everything out carefully on my futon: my mother's green capris, worn so often they had a soft, sueded texture; her matching green aloha shirt with coconut buttons; two pairs of clean underwear, pink and aqua; a satiny beige bra that had seen better days; worn white flip-flops; and, oddly, a pair of white cotton gloves with gold bands at the wrists. Two wrinkled pamphlets from the hospital were crumpled up at the bottom: "Speak Up," about how to be your own advocate and have a positive experience in the hospital, and "Pain Is a Sensation That Hurts." She'd also signed a sheaf of forms about "Patient Rights and Responsibilities," dated 7/6/07 in her classic textbook cursive. I realized, as I rubbed my fingers over the forms, that this was the last thing she ever wrote.

A soft, light scent rose from the clothes, and I could not for the life of me remember what kind of laundry soap she'd used. Not Tide: too expensive. Maybe Purex, or was it Gain? I could remember a big green bottle leaking blue down the neck, and a bottle of Downy with a pink lid next to it. Her clothes still smelled lotiony, peachy, with a hint of violet. When I laid the outfit on the futon, Martha immediately jumped up, circled around the aloha shirt, curled up on it, and fell asleep. Something broke in me then—maybe it was how hilarious I knew my mother would've found it—*me*, with a *dog*, on *her* clothes! Or maybe it was seeing her outfit, arranged so innocently, so faded and familiar, that brought a whole new wave of loss for me.

When she got dressed that morning, she would've had no idea it would be the last outfit she'd choose in her life. She'd probably chosen the clothes without thought, based purely on the weather and what was clean in the laundry basket. She hated summer and hated being hot. She was probably sweaty, in a rush, trying to get my slow-moving father going so they wouldn't be late for her 6:30 a.m. appointment in Minneapolis. She probably made sure to fill the cats' food and water dishes, made sure there was some kind of pasta salad or hotdish in the fridge that my father could eat when they got back.

When I rolled the clothes up, held them to my face, and sucked in the smell, it was too soft and delicious for me to fully take in.

I found another smaller bag full of her incidentals: a Fiskars scissors; Secret deodorant; an Avon lipstick; a Depends pad; nail clippers; two silver barrettes; a big pill caddy with ten multicolored pills for each day; and a book, Ann Hood's *The Knitting*

Circle. She was on page twenty-four; her hospital tag with name, date, and bar code was tucked inside as a bookmark. Ann Hood was one of my favorite writers! I had no idea my mother had even heard of her, but then, since it involved knitting, it wasn't surprising that my mother had found her way to the book.

Later, when I Googled Ann Hood, I discovered something serendipitous on her website. After her five-year-old daughter, Grace, had died from a strep infection, Ann Hood found herself unable to read or write. As a way to cope, she took up knitting, and by doing so, found herself in a whole new circle of women, which eventually gave her the strength and fortitude (and perhaps inspiration?) to write again. "Knitting, I believe, saved my life," she wrote.

Holding the book in my hands brought a tremendous sense of connection between my mother and me, as well as between me and other writers. I, too, couldn't read or write after losing my mother. I, too, had floundered in grief and lost my ability to use words. Ann Hood went on to write: "Sitting in various knitting circles, I slowly learned that knitting had rescued other women too. Bad marriages, illness, addiction—knitting gave comfort and even hope through life's trials."

She could just as well have been talking about my mother. Trapped in an unhappy marriage, limited by poverty and my father's alcoholism and neglect, she found great comfort and solidarity in sewing, quilting, and knitting, especially in the company of her female friends. It was something I'd always envied about my mother: the strong friendships she nurtured and cultivated with other women. Too often in my life I'd abandoned my close female friendships in favor of whatever needy, jealous boyfriend came along and demanded all of my time and attention. Not so with my mother. After realizing my father wanted only to drink beer, watch the Twins, and play the lottery, my mother began planning getaways with her girlfriends to quilting retreats. She'd tell me funny stories about riding the bus and always ending up next to the one person who was traveling alone and somehow managed to glom onto her. Of course, my mother didn't have the heart to turn anyone away, so she'd spend the weekend with this random person in tow, talking her arm off every step of the way. Her "niceness," combined with her inability to stand up for herself, were the two things that collectively drove me crazy. Almost to her dying day I would say, repeatedly and with impatience in my voice, "Mom, you simply have to learn to say no to people. You're too nice, and if you're too nice, you get walked all over. It's not good for you. People take advantage."

Though I knew she hated when I said that, I also knew she wouldn't change. She had an innate niceness gene, whereas I had developed an aloof gene that allowed me to flip my magazine coolly, so that any airplane seatmate would know I was in no mood to talk. My mother was the one who sat there with a bag of knitting, completely ready to spend the whole flight visiting with whomever happened to be seated next to her. Only later would I realize how much I'd been missing out on. Only later would I realize how my mother's openness to the people around her gave her stories I would never hear.

I found one last thing at the very bottom of the bag: her eyeglasses. They were wrapped in mounds of toilet paper, then shoved inside a Ziploc bag labeled with a purple Abbott-Northwestern sticker. I'd been saving the eyeglasses of dead loved ones ever since my friend, Barry, had died, followed by my grandparents, one by one. Whenever the difficult discussions came up about who would get what, I always sheepishly, a little awkwardly, asked for their eyeglasses. There was something about the sight of them, their ability to define in an instant an entire personality and attitude, that compelled me.

My friend Barry had died of AIDS in Hawaii while I was a PhD student there. Originally from South Dakota, the son of conservative, religious parents, and a rising photographer in Minneapolis, Barry had fled to Hawaii after his diagnosis. Lovers had betrayed him; friends had abandoned him. I came to know him through my longtime college friend Dave and his then-partner, Dack. All of us had somehow, oddly, ended up living in Hawaii.

Barry's parents loved him—that I knew. They sent cards with twenty-dollar bills tucked inside them, but they didn't support his "lifestyle choices." I would never forget Barry telling me, in many of our long, recorded conversations, how his mother had put it. "We love you," she'd say, "but we don't like what you do, who you've become, how you live."

For Barry, understandably, that wasn't good enough. The night he died, dark lesions covering his body, lungs rattling for air while fluid filled them, Dave and I could no longer stand to see him struggle, so we lowered his bed down, notch by notch. With each notch, the fluid overtook Barry's oxygen intake. The sound was more harrowing than a drowning, which was exactly what was happening. It was an act of mercy, explained to us by one of his more compassionate nurses, but while I understood that intellectually, I had a very hard time understanding my place in it when it should have been his family who had loved him ever since he was a tiny baby.

His bedroom was painted deep aubergine with white trim. The shades were drawn, but morning sunlight hit the soft blanket on his lap and softened everything. Eventually someone came to take his body away in a black bag, but for several minutes, hours maybe, Dave and I lay there on the floor on the zebra rug, holding hands, not talking, waiting for what—we didn't know. There was quietness to the death. We respected it by not talking. I had only known Barry since he'd moved to Hawaii just a few months earlier. And yet I had known him so well. Every week I biked over to his apartment and he told me stories of his past as a "kept man" of an older Brazilian lover in the rain forest, where water dripped on clay tiles and monkeys howled while they made love. I recorded everything on a Panasonic mini-recorder with plans to someday write a book about him. Just like Truman Capote, Barry had been raised by warm but fussy aunts. His Aunt Norma, who gave him fancy green drinking glasses and pretty teacups, was already a prominent figure in my mind. I was invested as a listener and recorder of a life fading fast.

Death sat with us in the room. We remained lying on the floor. It was a hot Hawaii morning, and mynah birds squawked outside the windows. Neither of us had anywhere we needed to be—not yet. At a certain point, Dave and I eventually sat up, fed the parrot swooping recklessly around the apartment, and got ourselves some coffee and clean clothes. But something had shifted. We had seen death close up, had even invited it by lowering the bed, notch by notch. How could we go on with our days, take exams, ride our bikes, write emails, after watching someone pass from life into death?

Holding the softly wrapped bag of my mother's eyeglasses all these years later reminded me of how I'd wanted to have Barry's eyeglasses, though I'd known they should go to his family. Eyeglasses could bring a face back in a second. Barry's bright blue eyes and bemused smirk. The way my mother's brown eyes sparkled. It's what everyone noticed. Her eyes, they said. They have such light, such shine, such a sense of fun. I unwrapped my mother's glasses from the tissue and put them on, but the blurry bifocal lines only distorted the world in front of me.

Birthday

I turn forty-one two weeks after my mom dies. Our New York friends Barb and John have a family cabin on Lake Owasco, and every year in mid-August we all go down for a long weekend with our kids. My birthday hits that weekend.

Everyone seems surprised I'm there, having just buried my mother, but what else can I do? The long solitary days of hiding in my bed haven't begun yet. That will come later.

Plus, it's my birthday. When Savoy, Barb's nine-year-old daughter, hands me my present, tiny glass dragonflies fall into my lap from a mound of pink tissue paper.

Something like electricity jolts through my body.

I cry.

Everyone seems nervous, so we eat cake.

Wrong Turn

After my mom died, all the things I still didn't know about her and her past began to overwhelm me. I wanted answers, stories, or secrets to help me figure things out, so I wrote letters to her two best friends, Barb and Laura, to see if they might be able to meet me for dinner next time I was in Minnesota. Luckily, they agreed to meet me at the Arlington Haus, an old brick restaurant with paneled walls and saloon doors.

What surprised me was how self-conscious I felt. There I was, a forty-five-year-old woman walking into a restaurant in my hometown, yet I could feel my face flush with shame, especially when I couldn't, at first, find Barb and Laura anywhere. All eyes locked on me, and I could almost hear people thinking: "Well, now, what would she be doing here in Arlington all by herself?"

But just as I started to panic, someone said from a crowded back table, "Well, now, isn't that Annie Panning?" His voice was made of gravel and cigarettes, and amazingly enough, he still wore the same thick glasses that magnified his big blue eyes: Stubby Brown, an old friend of my father's from his softball-playing days. His wife, Diane, said hello as well. "We sure miss your mom," she said. We exchanged pleasantries, but then I heard Barb and Laura call to me from the adjoining room.

They both looked soft and powdery, so familiar and Midwestern in their pastel tops and short feathered hair. We hugged. There was so much of my mother in them that it was all I could do not to cry.

I ordered the walleye and made a big deal out of it. "That's good Midwestern food, right?" I said. "I'm gonna be a real

Minnesotan tonight." When Barb admitted she didn't eat fish, I asked how she could live in the Land of 10,000 Lakes and not eat fish. She laughed, and said, "I know!" They both had Mudslides with whipped cream on top; I ordered a glass of Chardonnay.

Barb, who'd spent more time with my mother than Laura, instantly started telling stories. "Well, we used to clean houses together in the Cities," Barb said. "We hated it with a passion but we laughed so hard sometimes we thought we were absolutely gonna die. The very first day of cleaning, she went to one house and I went to the neighbors', and I got done first, so I went over there and she was scrubbing the floors. And I said, 'Are you not done yet?' and she looked up and she had two big wads of Kleenex hanging out of each nostril."

Barb and Laura both laughed, but I didn't get it. "Why?" I asked.

"Well, she was so nervous!" Barb said. "She was so nervous about the first day of the new job she got a nosebleed and didn't know what to do."

I remember my mother talking about her cleaning experiences, but her stories never seemed as hilarious as these did. When I'd come home from college, she'd tell me how one of the women she cleaned for had planted a twenty-dollar bill on the bathroom floor to see whether or not she'd take it. Or, how one of the families installed a security camera that watched her every move. Or, the family that would spot check behind the refrigerator to see if my mother had cleaned properly all the way back there.

Even though it was good to hear all the funny stories, I knew that cleaning houses was perhaps more complicated for my mother than it was for Barb. Even after he'd quit drinking, my father continued to be an addict, switching from alcohol to Ativan, which left him doped up and often unemployed. After cleaning rich people's houses all day, my mother would come home to her own messy house, a husband who barely spoke to her, and barely enough money to live on.

Barb continued. "There was one time the little hook on the vacuum cleaner got stuck in your mom's back pocket and so when she stood up, the vacuum cleaner was hanging off her butt. We laughed so hard! We'd get going on something and laugh so hard the people we were cleaning for would hear us and say, 'You should not have this much fun—this is a job!'"

Again, I wondered how much fun it had really been for my mother, but I listened, picking at my pallid, greasy walleye. I ordered another glass of wine.

Barb continued with what could only be described as mirth in her voice. "One day we were laughing so hard we actually crawled into the closet and closed the door because the people were home and we didn't want them to hear us." She trailed off, munching on a clam strip. "So we had lots of fun times. She was a good friend to have."

Although I enjoyed the stories about my mother, especially the idea of her, as an adult, sitting in a closet laughing with her best friend, what I really wanted to hear were some of the hard truths I might not have known about. "Surely she had some flaws?" I asked.

There was a notable pause after my question, during which I polished off my second glass of wine. I was driving—a rental car, no less—so I knew I had to stop. Still, I was more like my father than I probably cared to admit, and craved another.

"Well, she was way too kind," Laura finally said, "as far as your dad went." She speared some of her salad and held the fork in mid-air. Then she was quick to add, "Though it's really not a flaw."

"But it stood in the way of her own happiness," I said. "Don't you think?"

Barb offered me some deep-fried mushrooms from her combo platter because she didn't like them. Whether this was a stall on her part, I couldn't tell, though I happily collected the mushrooms on my plate and dipped them in ranch.

"This might not be very nice," Barb said, "but it's something we always laughed over, me and your mom. Your mom always said this over and over: 'I took a right turn when I should've taken a left. I took a right when I should've taken a left.' That changed her whole life, you know."

I asked what she thought that other direction would've been for my mother.

"Oh," Laura said with certainty, "she would've gone to college."

Then Barb took over again. "She wanted more. She wanted to be something. But then Lowell came into the picture. And he wowed her and he was just so different from your mom. It was like the bad-boy type thing."

The restaurant had shifted from a post-work happy-hour crowd to a Friday-night dinner crowd. The kitchen sizzled with fish fries and burgers; sudden bursts of laughter made it hard for me to hear our conversation.

"Lowell was wild," Barb said.

"He was also spoiled," Laura added.

This surprised me. There were a lot of words I'd use to describe my father, but "spoiled" wasn't among them. I asked what she meant.

"Well," Laura said. "He'd wreck a car and his dad would just buy him another one."

"Really?" I asked. This surprised me. Even though they weren't poor, my grandparents didn't seem like people who would, or could, do something like that.

Barb tried to explain further. "Well, your dad's parents were sort of strict about the rules. But the boys, especially your dad, seemed to be able to break them all the time and there weren't any consequences."

I wondered about this. I'd seen a therapist for several years who suggested that my father was a classic narcissist. I'd never considered that before, but he met all the criteria, especially the one about thinking only of himself at almost every turn. He certainly thought little about my mother or her happiness, which again led me back to the question: "Why do you think my mother stayed with him?"

"She didn't know where to go," Barb said.

"I think she thought she couldn't make it on her own," Laura added.

Barb continued. "And she always said, 'I can't go home.' And she couldn't, not to Hank and Lou. Because, you know, your grandma was very judgmental. She was like, 'You made your bed, now lie in it.' Plus, I don't think Hank would've taken her in with you four kids."

I considered this, but still wondered why she'd never kicked my father out of the house. It wasn't like he was supplying her with a steady income or doing any parenting or household duties. I asked Barb and Laura why she never did.

"I'll tell you why," Barb said. "She couldn't kick Lowell out of the house because his dad owned it! She didn't have an out."

"Ah," I said. When my parents had finally moved from the trailer court to the Victorian house on Main, I knew they'd gotten help from my father's parents, but I was never clear on the particulars. Now it made sense. My mother was not only financially unstable on her own, but the very house she lived in didn't belong to her in any way.

I was getting riled up, which happened every time I learned more about my parents' difficulties, especially my mom's. Barb and Laura sensed this, I think, and tried to calm me down. Laura reached her hand across the table, and patted it. "But you know what, Anne? I think your dad totally adored your mom. He absolutely adored her—"

"But he didn't show it," I said.

"Right," she said, and patted the table again.

"Didn't she ever get mad, though?" I asked. "Really pissed off? I mean, didn't she ever let you see that side of her?"

Barb smiled. "Well, many times she said, 'I could take a frying pan and hit him right now!' It was hard on her. Here four little kids are looking at you hungry and Dad's sitting in the chair passed out. You know his barber shop was attached to a bar, so he'd cut a few haircuts, go have a few drinks, cut a few haircuts, go have a few drinks. Then he'd come home with no money."

As Barb told it, everything imploded when my father failed to file income taxes several years in a row, and, of course, got busted. They were forced to pay back taxes, which they were unable to do, so eventually his wages were garnished, leaving them with nothing to live on. They had to go on welfare and medical assistance, and never really managed to crawl out of poverty after that.

"And did you know," Barb said, "when your mom got food stamps, she would not use them in Arlington. She'd drive to another town."

I remember feeling a similar shame when I used my special free lunch tickets at school because of our below-poverty-level income.

Laura looked at me oddly. "I'm sorry, but I just keep staring at your hands," she said. "They're exactly like your mother's. It's the darndest thing."

I looked down at my hands. This was what I missed living in New York—very few people there had ever known or even met my mother.

We stayed so long that the dinner crowd had now cleared out, leaving us with a bit more peace and quiet. I kept saying that it was probably time to go, but they kept telling more stories and I loved hearing them. How they called themselves "The Big Butt Sisters." How once on a trip to the Amana Amish colony they all got out their swimsuits and they were exactly the same suit ("the same ugly blue floral in jumbo size from Wal-Mart!" Barb said). How once in Chicago a taxi driver had ripped them off and driven them all over the city in circles. ("What?" Laura said. "Did we have STUPID written on our foreheads?") How once they went to a Mystery Dinner in Spicer and worried that everyone thought they were lesbians. The stories went on and on, and as I listened, I smiled, grateful to hear how much fun she'd had, how much laughter and silliness they'd shared, how lifesaving that must have been for my mother.

As we wound down, there was one last story Barb said they absolutely had to tell me, about when my mother was in the ICU and didn't seem to be getting better. "We had been planning a cruise to Mexico," Barb said. "And we knew of course your dad would never go because he wouldn't fly. So when we came to visit her in the ICU, Laura told your mom, 'Barb, if you get better, we're taking you on a cruise to Mexico, and we'll pay for your trip. So you have to get better so you can come with us.'"

I remembered the story vaguely.

"Anyway, of course your mom never got better," Barb said. "So I'm sitting on the plane to Mexico and a lady came up and sat by me, and Anne, she looked just like your mother. She dressed like your mom—same blue jeans and sweatshirty type thing on. And we started visiting and I told her, 'You remind me of my friend who passed away this summer' and I kinda told her all about it and it turns out the lady herself was in the ICU at Abbott that past summer on the third floor—"

"Which is exactly where my mom was!" I said.

"I know!" Barb said. "Anyway, she had just learned to quilt, and I looked back at Laura and I said, 'Look back and tell me who you think that looks like,' and of course she couldn't believe it. She looked just like Barb and everything about her was like Barb."

Laura, calmer and more subdued, continued. "So anyway, later, when we got on the ship, we were sitting at a table on deck and all of the sudden these dragonflies started swarming above us. I mean, swarming."

Barb laughed. "Out in the middle of the ocean!"

"And people were looking at us, like, what is going on?" Laura said. "And we both said, 'Barb is here.' Your mother was with us, one way or the other."

After we said goodbye and went our separate ways, I drove down Main Street past our old house, the front porch dappled with dark shadows from the streetlights.

Once the funeral was over and everyone had gone their separate ways, I had a hard time adjusting to my life again back in New York. Hudson approached me warily at first, as if I might break. Lily seemed wittier and savvier, singing and dancing and performing every time I entered a room, to keep the mood light.

Mark gave me wide berth to cry, retreat, sleep, wander off if I needed to. But where would I go? What would I do? Everything seemed to require more energy than I was able to summon. To make matters worse, I had to start teaching in a couple weeks, and had no idea how I was going to manage being a lively and engaged person in front of students day after day.

All I could manage to do was watch bits of television. The Food Network was soothing, and I came to love Giada DeLaurentiis. Even scrappy little Bobby Flay grew on me, and I loved watching him barbecue with his friends and talk about serrano peppers. But if I ever tried to watch a real TV show, I found it pointless. Who cared if Robin couldn't get a date on *How I Met Your Mother*? So what if Jim tricked Dwight again on *The Office*? I craved tenderness and sincerity, not wryness or irony. I spent my time with the kids, reading or coloring, and occasionally walked along the Erie Canal listening to violin adagios on my iPod.

Soon there was less than a week before classes would begin, and I knew I wasn't ready to face it all. I decided to ask for a reduced teaching load, going from three classes to one, a creative nonfiction workshop with only nine students, which seemed manageable. With a small class, I could be honest with them if I had to. If I had a rough day, I could step away, or even cancel.

The weeks blurred by. When the snow began to fall and the cold crept into the corners of our old Victorian, all I could manage most days was to wrap myself up in the wedding quilt my mother had made me. Often I'd just lie there, bundled up inside the quilt like an infant, and stare out my bedroom window at the dark bare maple trees.

The students in my class that semester became a significant part of my grieving process. I rarely shared personal information with my students, but this time it felt right. One woman, Ashley, had flashy dark eyes and dark hair and rode horses somewhere east of Rochester almost every day. She wrote so beautifully it buoyed me.

Another student, Matt, brought in essays about his father, who'd recently come out as gay and caused tremendous family problems, especially for his depressive mother. Matt, like Ashley, wrote with empathy and compassion. He took risks and submitted essays about his family that broke my heart in the best of ways.

I'll never forget sitting in our tiny basement classroom that winter with those students, watching the snow fly outside, talking quietly about what makes a good essay: sincerity, vulnerability, a desire to connect with others through stories of pain, truth, and honesty.

Thanks to that workshop, I managed to write a short piece about losing my mother.

so

I have parasailed in Malaysia—so what? My mother died days later in a high-tech Minneapolis hospital. I flew back: suntanned, frantic. The nurses hung a piece of gauze soaked in peppermint oil above her bed to mask the smell of death. I cannot forget the smell. Or hanging above Penang Bay in my black swimsuit—warm wind rushing my sails, white lip of beach biting into blue. My two bare legs dangled dangerously. From below, my small children watched and waved, squinting. When I landed, legs bicycling through sand, a woman from England congratulated me for my bravery. "I could never do that," she said. "That's what I thought," I said. But up in the sky someone else was already lifting off. A Muslim woman in black burka hung high under a rainbow parachute—free.

Dusty Rose

At the Brockport public library, I find an old book for sale for twenty-five cents. After settling into a chair by the window, I read that in the Victorian era, people captured butterflies to use as decorations in their homes because their colors were so brilliant and beautiful. Some butterflies were especially treasured for their saturated colors: deep orange, lemon yellow, bright blue, Chinese red. Mounted carefully under glass with fine silver pins, the colors, it said, would last forever.

But dragonflies, the author reports, are different. They lose their color almost immediately after death.

The coloration of living dragonflies is infinitely varied and often surprisingly beautiful. But alas! Some of it fades badly in preserved specimens. The surface colors keep very well, as does the iridescence of the clear wing membrane, but the deeper pigment colors suffer from drying. Greens fade to yellow, purples to black, and bright blues darken with internal post-mortem changes.

—Dragonflies of North America, 1955

I think of the wedding quilt my mother made me almost twenty years ago. Each bright block fades a bit more each season. One of the blue calicos has gone from a deep navy to a powder blue. A bright pink daisy print from a childhood dress looks creamy and worn, the pink now more dusty rose than fuchsia.

Sometimes, to preserve its colors, I wrap the quilt in tissue paper and place it carefully in my mother's old cedar chest at the foot of my bed.

Red Heart Balloon

When my mother's death anniversary came around every summer, I never quite knew what to do. Not to mark the occasion seemed too sad, but dragging myself and others through the grief again was also hard. On one particular July 27, an epic heat wave gripped the entire East Coast. Most people closed up their houses, pulled the shades, and checked out. An eerie haze hung in the air like smoke. Despite the heat, I wanted to do something special to mark the date, so I pulled on my biking clothes and went to the garage to gear up for a ride.

I had no specific destination in mind; it didn't matter *where* I went but *that* I went. But I could feel something pulling me south of Brockport—past the Taco Bell and McDonald's, past Wegmans and Island Tan, through the ongoing construction on Highway 19. But just before I headed up the hill (the only hill in Brockport, actually), I found myself pulling into the Sweden Corners strip mall and parking in front of Dollar Tree.

I went in. "I'll take that red heart balloon," I said, pointing to number twenty-five in their helium balloon display.

"Well, you sure decide fast," the clerk said as she tightened it around the nozzle and blew it up. "Most people stand around and take forever deciding."

She asked if I wanted a weight to hold it down, but when I told her I was on my bike, she seemed a little nervous. "A helium balloon on a bike?" she said. "Never heard of that." But I felt no need to explain; I was on a mission.

I passed Country Max, the Golden Eagle Diner, and Dollinger's Hotel, which had just months ago been a Holiday Inn Express. At the peak of the hill, I saw the little cow statue that marked the Sweden Farmers Museum before finally coming upon the huge, sprawling Lakeview Cemetery. I'd driven past the cemetery for years but never had occasion to enter.

I turned in.

Growing up, my bedroom had overlooked a cemetery, so graveyards didn't bother me. This one was gorgeous with rolling hills, huge shade trees, and a pond surrounded by weeping willows. I sat on a stone bench and thought: *Here I am.* I wanted to feel something. I tied the red balloon to the handlebar of my bike and watched it bob against the blue sky. I wondered if my siblings were doing anything to mark the day, but then I realized that they were all at work. I was the only one with summers off, but I also seemed to be the one who wanted to talk about our mother's death the most. My siblings didn't exactly resist the subject when I mentioned it, but they also didn't want to dwell on it like I did. It made sense; why would you want to focus on something that brought up so much heartache and pain? One night at Amy's, we'd been watching TV with our brothers when I brought it up.

As if on cue, Jim wandered outside for a cigarette. Mike disappeared out to his truck to go "grab something." Amy turned up the volume on the TV when Maisie and Zoe started barking.

Amy has said she doesn't want to feel sad all the time. "I like to remember all the good times and how lucky I was to have such a good mother for as long as I got her. Why keep going over the negative stuff all the time?"

Yes, I got that. I understood exactly where she was coming from.

Still, I found myself unable to stop.

Why? Was it because I lived so far away, and always had? Was it because I regretted how much time I'd spent away from my mother? Was it guilt? Or was it because, as my siblings sometimes claimed, I was a drama queen and felt the need to make a huge big deal out of everything? Once, Mike had called me out on it. "God, Anne," he'd said. "Everything has to be such a big drama for you. 'Oh, this is *the* best barbecue chicken I've ever had!' or 'This is *the* most humid day ever!' Isn't anything just normal or whatever for you?"

Maybe. Or maybe not.

I got my cell phone out and took a photo of the red balloon bobbing in the air, making sure to capture the background of the cemetery. I texted the photo to Amy, Mike, and Jim, along with the message, "Thinking of Mom."

I waited. No one texted back. Again, they were all at work. What did I expect? I closed my eyes, breathing in the humid air. I waited for a sign, but all I could think of was how hot and miserable I was, how I wished I'd brought more water to drink, how the cemetery—though beautiful and peaceful—was not *my* cemetery.

I headed south, turning on Shumway, and came upon a huge alfalfa field. It seemed a good place to stop. After making sure there were no cars coming, I untied the balloon from my handlebars, looked up, and let it go. I vowed to watch the balloon until it was completely out of sight, and then—maybe then—my mother would give me a sign.

But as I was peering up at the sky, a movement out of the corner of my eye distracted me. On a tall, thorny weed right next to me sat a dragonfly. I froze. It stayed right beside me, bobbing a bit in the wind.

When I looked up, searching the entire sky to find the balloon, it was gone.

On a late Friday afternoon in September, I meet my friend, Sarah, for happy hour at Salena's in Rochester. The sun, a warm buttery gold, is so beautiful it makes me want to cry. We've been in the middle of a massive heat wave, and this is one of the nicest days in months. We sit outside with Coronas and limes and talk about the new hairstylist we both share, how good she is at color and highlights. I've just had mine done and we both say it looks natural, like the sun did it.

Soon my friend pulls a gift out of her purse. It's a yellow cellophane gift bag tied off with a gold ribbon.

"What?" I say. It's not my birthday, nor am I celebrating anything. It's just a regular old day.

"Open it," she says.

Inside is a pair of socks. They're black with purple, green, and blue dragonflies scattered over them. They're soft and creamy.

"Oh," I say, an electric charge running through my whole body, right down to my toes. "Thank you! I don't have any dragonfly socks. These are so beautiful."

I clutch them to my chest and get choked up. A dragonfly gift is someone remembering my mother, remembering that it still hurts, remembering how much I miss her.

I tuck the socks in my bag.

We order another round as the sun slants west.

No Trespassing

A couple of years after my mom died, things started going badly for my dad. It had started with general forgetfulness, confusion, weird behaviors, and grew from there. To put it more bluntly, my dad had started to completely lose it, so after hashing things out with Amy, I flew to Minnesota, where we went to check on his house. We'd both received notices that there'd been several missed payments—more than several— and things didn't look good. As Amy turned off Main Street onto Alden, I saw the cast iron skillet my mother had hand-painted with their address, 301, still hanging on the front porch. I reminded myself to grab it this time. The grass was overgrown and shaggy, and my father's black Buick still sat parked in the driveway, its battery dead. The willow tree had gone untrimmed for so long that its branches now drooped completely to the ground and made it look like a strange little hut. My mother used to love to sit and sew underneath the willow tree, a glass of sweet iced tea by her side, her toenails polished pale peach.

As Amy parked in front of the house, I saw that the roof was so far gone that it was mossy, the shingles curled up like eyelashes. The old dog kennel at the side of the house was filled with inoperable lawnmowers. Beyond that, I noticed wet cardboard boxes full of broken tools, old hunting jackets and camo hats, rusty golf clubs, and a cracked lawn fertilizer cart.

As Amy and I approached the house, there it was—what I'd been expecting and dreading: a foreclosure sign taped to the front door.

```
┌─────────────────────────────────────────┐
│                                         │
│               WARNING                   │
│            NO TRESPASSING!               │
│   ANY PERSON(S) DEFACING THE PROPERTY    │
│         OR CAUGHT TRESPASSING            │
│        WILL BE PROSECUTED TO THE         │
│       FULLEST EXTENT OF THE LAW.         │
│                                         │
└─────────────────────────────────────────┘
```

Because of his encroaching dementia and erratic, sometimes dangerous behavior, my father had been deemed unfit to live alone and had been living in Autumn Lane Memory Care Center in Gaylord. There had been several episodes that had led to this point, including him trying to start his truck with a screwdriver, nearly burning his assisted living apartment down by leaving a pan on the stove, and calling the sheriff to report that men in white were sitting on his bed trying to kill him. He'd run the gamut of social services: emergency psych wards, Meals on Wheels, a halfway house, assisted living, free county mental health services. The problem was, because of his relatively young age and his otherwise good physical health, no one really knew what to do with him. The memory care center had been the last option, the last place that had a spot for someone with no money or resources. It wasn't ideal; he was easily the youngest one in there by ten or even twenty years, but the doors were locked down at all times, and he needed that kind of security. He wasn't very happy about it, and neither were we, but at least he was safe, fed, and taking his medications.

As a result of all this upheaval, the mortgage on his house had gone unpaid for months. A real estate agent had listed the house, claiming she was very familiar with "these situations."

Still, because of its rough condition, the house had sat on the market and eventually went into foreclosure. Here and there, we'd tried to move out all the things we could, but with all of us scattered around, it was hard to ever really do a full clean-out (especially given my parents' hoarder tendencies).

I cupped my hands and peeked inside the kitchen door; the first thing I noticed was the Raggedy Ann cookie jar sitting on the counter. How had we missed that? Next to it sat crumpled McDonald's bags and empty beer bottles left behind from the last time we'd cleaned out. Everything looked hazy through the screen, but I could still see the familiar apple wallpaper border, the ancient electric can opener under the cupboard, the old-fashioned kitchen sink with separate hot and cold faucets.

Amy and I tried the door; she still had my parents' house key after all this time, but the locks had been changed. "What should we do?" I asked. "We have to get in there one last time." Even though I was older than Amy by three years, I sometimes looked to her as the grown-up who would take charge.

"Let's break in," she said. But when she tried shoving open the windows, they were locked, too.

"Shit," I said.

"Come on," Amy said. I followed her around the side of the house, ducking under the clothesline.

Amy yanked at the screen of my mother's sewing room, but it was stuck tight. "Wait! I got it!" she said. She threw the screen onto the grass and pushed open the window. But it was high—higher than we could get into without help.

"Here," I said. "Let me try."

Amy gave me a boost and I tumbled forward onto my mother's sewing desk. I grabbed Amy's hands and helped pull her through the white embroidered curtains, and, finally, into the room. Once in, she posed triumphantly, and I pulled out my cell phone to take her picture. Later, looking at it, what surprised me was how happy she looked—a big smile on her face, sunglasses propped on her head, mischief twinkling in her eyes.

Amy and I both had to pee, but when we went into the bathroom, we found black and yellow tape wrapped around the toilet like a crime scene. WINTERIZED, it said. The sinks, too, had been sealed off. I had to go so badly I found an old ice cream pail and peed in it while crouching in a corner.

Amy walked around the house, crossing her legs and bouncing up and down. "You're welcome to use this," I said, and showed her the pail full of pee.

"Oh my God," she said. "Gross."

This was how sisters spent time together, I thought, or at least it's how we did.

There was really nothing good left in the house. We'd already taken the few nice pieces of furniture our parents had inherited. Long ago, we kids had discussed at length who would get what: the pie cupboard and 1940s enamel wood-fire stove would go to Mike; the old barn cupboard and Moderntone dishes would be Amy's; the wood box and my great grandmother's tall maple dresser would be mine. Though he was the oldest and we gave him ample opportunity, Jim never asked for a single thing, even when pressed. "I don't care," he'd say. "It's not like I really have anywhere to put anything anyway," which was true. He lived in back of Mike's property in a kind of open-ended arrangement that had lasted for years.

I found a few random things: a linen tablecloth with embroidered violets; a garlic press; a Lutheran church cookbook; my father's sobriety pins from AA; a box of my father's old barber supplies, including a bottle of Hair Milk along with his original shaving mug and brush. But then something caught my eye in a corner: a pink teapot shaped like a beaded purse. I grabbed its delicate handle, rubbed it clean against my T-shirt, and held it up to the light. The pink pearlescent finish glowed milky and soft in the light diffused through lace curtains. It was a hidden treasure, and, afraid I'd break it, I went out to the van and tucked it into a safe corner, nestled in a pile of blankets.

I trudged upstairs to my old bedroom. My parents' collapsed canopy bed lay on the floor in pieces, as well as bundles of old greeting cards my mother had saved from every single occasion, tied off with satin ribbons.

I heard Amy digging around in her old bedroom, and went check on her.

"Don't you want this?" Amy asked. She held up my old high school varsity jacket, black wool with orange trim. I remembered saving up my babysitting money for months to afford it. An orange cursive "Anne" slanted at the front pocket. White cat hair, thick as a blanket, coated the entire thing.

"I don't think so," I said. I'd stood in front of it and debated it before, but now that Amy offered it to me, it seemed wrong to leave it behind.

"Really?" Amy said. "You should take it."

"It's full of cat hair," I said. "Mark's allergies will go crazy."

"Just roll it up and stick it in a garbage bag," Amy said. She knelt on the floor and looked up at me. With her white-blonde hair and bright green eyes, Amy was a bright light among our family's dark eyes and dark hair. Although we had a good relationship now, it still made me feel terrible—what a mean older sister I'd been as we were growing up. When we were little, I would tease her that she was adopted, claiming that Mom and Dad had told me but it was a secret. I'd scare her about the cemetery our bedroom windows faced and told her ghosts of the dead would get us while we were asleep. As a teenager, I wouldn't let her borrow my clothes, stating that it would ruin my individuality. Now, I looked at her face, as familiar to me as my own, and thought of how we'd aged and settled into ourselves over the years. On a trip to Chicago recently, she'd bought some Clinique product she said would make a faint age spot (one I couldn't even see) disappear. When I argued that it was all a ruse, she'd said, "No. Come and see me in three months. You'll be surprised." Recently, I'd noticed an age spot on my cheek and wished I could make it disappear.

In her old childhood bedroom, I looked at my sister and wanted to say, "Amy, you're amazing. You're beautiful. You've been through so much and your heart is still so good and pure." I wanted to kiss her soft slightly freckled cheek, and ask her to forgive me for being such a cruel older sister all those years ago.

"Here," I said. "Give me the jacket." I rolled up the hair-covered jacket in an old sheet and carried it under my arm like a sleeping bag.

Our last stop was the upstairs bathroom that our mother had made cozy by wallpapering the sloped wall over the tub in a tiny floral print, painting the vanity and chair a soft strawberry pink, and glazing flower patterns on the side of the claw-foot tub. It still smelled like her Caress soap.

"I wish I could take that tub," I said. "That's what I really want."

"Yeah," Amy said. "I know."

We stood there silently, unsure what to do next.

"Let's get out of here," I said.

As we shuffled down the hallway, I noticed there were still several old paper dolls framed and hanging on the walls. I thought about taking them, but I already had so many. At a certain point, I realized, you had to let go.

I hauled my things out to the van, and came back inside for one last look. In my mom's sewing room, I found an embroidered wall hanging, red stitches on muslin bordered by calico: *Love Me, Love My Cat*. I took it, though I didn't have cats and didn't plan to get one. My mother had hand-stitched this. It could not be left behind.

I took my seat in Amy's minivan and, hands folded in my lap, didn't look back as we drove away.

At Big Lots, I'm shopping for a Rubbermaid tote but get distracted by something in the clearance aisle: a burnished copper dragonfly memorial marker with prismatic glass eyes and an ornately scrolled banner that reads "In Memory of Mother."

It's eighty percent off.

It's $1.40.

When I try to pack it in my suitcase for my trip to Minnesota, it doesn't fit. It's too big, too unwieldy, too leggy and sharp for airplane travel.

Instead, I go to Bittersweet, one of my favorite Brockport shops, and buy a pewter dragonfly charm about the size of my hand. It's pounded and pierced in circle and spiral patterns and the texture feels good under my fingertips.

It's from Guatemala.

It's $12.98.

I fold it inside a soft T-shirt, tuck it into my suitcase, and fly away to Minnesota, where I place it on my mother's gravestone, still covered with morning dew.

If there's one thing I've learned, it's that in my family nothing holds. Trauma nips at our heels like a lost kitten. Peace is fleeting and illusory. One morning, just three years after my mother died, my father ate a small breakfast at Autumn Lane Memory Care Center, walked back to his room, fell to the floor and went into cardiac arrest. I'd been up at my office preparing for a full day of classes when Mark came running in, breathless. "Annie," he said. "It's your dad."

Oddly, when I heard the words "cardiac arrest," I did not immediately think "death." However, the looks Mark gave me as we frantically gathered my things and sped out the door indicated this would not end well. Within a couple hours, I again found myself on a plane to Minnesota. I'd become a veteran of sudden traumatic flights home, and sat there quietly in my seat looking out at the brilliant blue mid-September sky.

I sometimes find myself telling people that my father died of grief, but I wonder if that's fair, or accurate, or whether it instead provides a way for me to add a dramatic flourish to an otherwise sad and inexplicable occurrence. For years I waded through my mother's medical files, trying to make sense of her death. I became a rookie expert on all matters of the body, on critical care, on bladder sling surgery, on hastily written doctors' notes and conflicting diagnoses, though none of it ever explained to me why my mother had died. Not really.

But for someone to simply fall over and die, like my father had? There was very little sense to make of that, either—save for the fact that he had gone crazy after my mother's death.

And when I say "crazy," I mean crazy, as in he once thought people were sitting on his bed and plotting to kill him. "Crazy" as in he'd call me randomly, day or night, and say things like, "When are you picking me up for the wedding?" when there was no wedding. "Crazy" as in I watched him once in a hospital neurology unit sit on the floor, pick at the tiles, and exclaim what a cute train he was playing with.

My father's psychotic break is really too much to process here, though. I'd have to peel back years of his alcoholism, prescription drug abuse, depression, and anxiety to uncover the reasons for his complete psychological collapse. But since my father's problems have always overshadowed everything and everyone in our family, I find myself resisting. I keep telling myself: this is my mother's story, not his. But of course their stories are so entwined they're impossible to separate.

Amy and I have joked that our mother would've rolled her eyes at our father's sudden "craziness." "Of course it's always all about him," our mother would've said. "Here I am, the one who died, and he's still complaining about the fact that he can't sleep and he never feels good and can't get his act together. Typical." At times we even wondered if our father was acting, or at least milking, some of his ailments, in order to get the attention he so craved.

I even vowed, as I was finishing this book, not to include any mention of his death. How could I allow his death to shift the attention away from my mother's story? Not only were we all constantly running, driving, and flying in a panic to "save" him at a moment's notice, but he'd also stolen important grieving time that should've been devoted to my mother. Even in death, he dominated everyone's attention. Even in death, he continued to steal focus from my mother.

But of course that's no way to look at your father's unexpected and tragic death. And as time passed without having a mother or a father, I began to see that life wasn't going to behave in the orderly, tidy way I wanted it to. His sudden death bled over into her death, which I was (and still am) trying to process. How could we all take on any more grief? And good God, what had happened to him anyway?

Aside from his mental and psychological deterioration, his body was as physically strong and strapping as it'd always been. In fact, after so many unexplained episodes, we'd finally brought him to Mayo Clinic for a full two-day comprehensive battery of tests—everything from EKG to EEG to MRI to blood work to a four-hour neurological exam to a CT scan to a sleep disorder consult. At the end of all the testing, we gathered in Dr. Choi's office. His job was to help give us—finally—a diagnosis. But what was the diagnosis we had waited so long to hear? "Undetermined." It seems he had an underlying brain problem, or a "neurodegenerative problem." When we asked what exactly that meant, the doctor said it was likely a form of dementia, maybe Lewy body, and that we were in for a long and probably difficult haul. "The best we can do," she said, "is try and adjust his meds and see how it goes. But really, there's no urgency at this point."

Two weeks later, he died.

After my father died, I found myself stuck in a logjam of grief, kind of like when your drain gets clogged and nothing can get in or out. Both of my relatively young and relatively healthy parents had suddenly died, leaving me orphaned at age forty-four. Plus, because my parents had no money and no power of attorney or a living will, every week I received stacks of my father's unpaid heating, electricity, water, and numerous credit card bills, and had no idea what to do with them. I made a special folder titled "Dad's Unpaid Bills," which grew fatter and fatter with each passing month. Eventually, collection agencies started calling me. I would answer, listen briefly, then say the same thing over and over again: "My dad is dead. And I'm not paying these bills." Luckily a lawyer friend had informed me that I was in no way responsible or accountable for my father's debt; none of us were.

Still the calls and bills came, eventually threatening legal action if steps weren't taken to rectify the situation. In addition to that, their house stood practically rotting with neglect as one season slipped into the next. Because of the red tape of foreclosure and the house's ratty condition, no one was even looking at it, much less putting in an offer. I called the real estate agent regularly, whose weary voice suggested to me that she'd completely given up on it. Amy and I spoke on the phone constantly, trying to coordinate our efforts from afar. Our stress levels ran high, and we both agreed that dealing with the aftermath of our father's death was like having a second full time job. In addition to managing a busy family, I tried to stay on top of everything, but every now and then, one of my mother's stray medical bills would arrive in the mail, and I'd stop in my tracks, undone.

At around that same time, out of the blue (or so I thought), I was struck down by a blindingly painful headache. I'd never had such an extreme headache before, and was in so much pain that I literally couldn't get out of bed. Mark kept trying to get me to go to the doctor, but I kept vomiting and thought my head would explode. Things went from bad to worse (we had house guests), and when I ended up in the ER, none of the doctors could figure out why a healthy, active woman in her early forties would be suddenly struck down with a headache like this. Did I have a brain tumor? Meningitis? I had a spinal tap. I had a CT scan. I had an MRI. Test after test revealed nothing. The doctors kept scratching their heads. I was eventually given a prescription for Imitrex, a migraine medication, and released with instructions to take the meds as soon as I felt the onset of another headache.

And I did get migraines again, one of them so severe that I had to be hospitalized overnight. I was on such heavy painkillers that I could hardly speak when Mark brought the kids to see me. The doctors were again uncertain as to why I would suddenly be struck with migraines. They said migraines usually began in your twenties, that there's usually a history. To start this late was unusual. They sent me to a neurologist, who had me touch my nose with my fingers, walk in a straight line, and hop on one foot. Again, nothing out of the ordinary. But thankfully he lingered with me a while; perhaps I was his last patient of the day. He asked question after question, and it was his final one that finally cracked the case. "Have you had any deeply troubling or traumatic experiences lately?"

"No," I said. But then I thought: did losing both of your parents in five years count as troubling or traumatic? I explained to him about their deaths, and he instantly began nodding his head and writing something down. "The body is not a machine," he said. "Your emotions are not stand-alone. This is your body's reaction to grief, and it's important that you're treated on a physical as well as a psychological level." He asked if I'd been seeing a therapist. When I told him I stopped therapy after my mother died, he scowled. "That's not good. You should go back. That's a lot for anyone to process, much less someone who suffers from depression."

And so I did go back, and talked it out, and talked it out. Mostly I talked about my mother, how much regret I felt for all the years I'd spent living so far away from her. "I feel like I abandoned her," I kept saying. Of course I'd been doing interesting things, going to graduate school, traveling the world, and building a career. My mother never took any of that away from me; I know she was proud of my accomplishments, but I also know she had wished for it to be otherwise. "I'm just happiest when you kids are all right here," she used to say on the rare occasions when we were.

The fact is, I absolutely had to leave in order to survive and thrive, and somehow, thanks to therapy, I came to understand that. At age seventeen, fresh out of high school, I joined a summer theatre company, moved away, and didn't look back for a long, long time. I remember my grandparents drove my mother and me all the way up to Ely, Minnesota, to drop me off. As my mother helped me unload my Raggedy Ann quilt and single suitcase of clothes, I remember her saying something like, "You with your big dreams, Annie." It wasn't said in a derogatory manner, but in a bemused, almost wistful way. I wanted to be a Broadway actress! I was going to college! I had a boyfriend who looked like Billy Idol! I was ready to fly away, and even though I knew I'd miss her, I was all about my own sparkling future that spread itself before me with possibilities.

It must have been so hard for her to see me go.

I still think about my mother every day, though more impressionistically than concretely. It's as if her memory is woven into the fabric of my days. When Hudson came home from school last week with a pillowcase he'd sewn in Home Ec, my first and only thought was how excited my mother, a seamstress, would've been. When I broke my nose recently by running into a glass wall, my very first impulse was to call her. I craved how much she'd tease me. "Annie, how in the heck did you run into a glass wall?" But I also craved the way she'd comfort and mother me. "Oh, you poor thing."

People always say how hard it is after a loved one dies, when they can no longer remember the sound of that person's voice. But for me, it's the opposite. I can still hear my mother's voice so clearly, the sound of her tired chuckle when she was only half-listening, the high-pitched way she'd talk to her cats, the way she'd try to pep up the end of her sentences when she was having a hard day: "But it'll all be okay, *right*?" I especially remember coming home from a long day at work and listening to her voice on our answering machine. "Hi Annie. It's Mom. I didn't really want anything. Just calling because. . . I don't know. . . no real reason. Okay, well. Give the kids a big hug from Grandma."

I knew her so well. Her "I didn't really want anything" always meant that she was lonely and most likely frustrated with my father and really just wanted someone to hear her out and maybe make her laugh. I was almost always willing to provide that for her, even if it was from a distance. Now, whenever Amy and I leave each other phone messages, we still use our mother's famous line, "Well, I didn't really want anything. . ." when of course we still want so much.

The "goneness" of my mother is the hardest thing to explain or even to understand myself. There's the goneness of her physical body, which was cremated; to this day, I still regret not keeping some of her ashes for myself. I don't know what exactly I would've done with them. Put them in a lovely clay jar on the mantel? Sprinkled them in my backyard? Tossed them up to the dragonflies? But her *essence* being gone, irrevocably, is the hardest. Her primary spot in my life—gone. Having someone in my corner, no matter what—gone. The one person in the world I could "brag" to without bragging—gone. The person to whom I want to report every single thing that happens to me, good or bad—gone. Also, as I mother my own children, I feel her absence even more acutely with each milestone the kids reach.

The other day Lily lost a tooth, and put it under her pillow that night. I was on Tooth Fairy duty, and although I had two dollars ready to stash under her pillow, I could not for the life of me find the tooth. I left the money anyway. The next morning Lily grilled me about why the Tooth Fairy hadn't taken her tooth, and I made up something stupid, which seemed to satisfy her for the time being. But I remember thinking later: had this ever happened to my mother? What other parental foibles might she have shared with me as the years went on? What, for her, were the hardest parts of raising us? The funniest? The trickiest?

I keep her present in our lives by placing photographs all around the house. One of the things I loved about living in Asia was how everyone kept shrines for their dead—usually a huge photograph in a gold frame, an orange stuck with incense, gold coins, chopsticks so they would never be hungry in the next life. I don't exactly keep a shrine to my mother, although some might argue otherwise. I like to have her around. I need to see and remember her face.

One of my favorite pictures of my mother sits on the windowsill above the kitchen sink, where I see it all the time. It's an old faded Kodachrome with a white border. In the photo, my mother must be sixteen, seventeen years old. She's kneeling in her parents' yard, wearing blue jeans and a red sweater. It's autumn, the slanted afternoon light brushing her shoulders, maple leaves scattered all around. She's holding their cat, looking off to the side; she smiles at someone outside the frame. The sun is on her face. Her golden blonde hair blows in the breeze as she waits for the next moment of her life. You can almost feel the warmth of that autumn day, and of her, right in the middle of it.

Acknowledgements

Special thanks to the following literary journals in which some of this memoir, in various versions, first appeared: *Brevity: A Journal of Concise Literary Nonfiction* and *Waccamaw: A Journal of Contemporary Literature*.

Thanks also to the following retreats/residencies that provided time and space to work on this book: Constance Saltonstall Foundation for the Arts, Ithaca, New York, and Wellspring House, Ashland, Massachusetts.

I was fortunate to have some very generous readers during the early stages of writing this book. Special thanks to June Spence, Gail Hosking, and Phil Young, who read early drafts of the manuscript and provided smart, detailed feedback and suggestions that helped make the book much stronger. I know how much time it takes to read and critique a fledgling manuscript in progress and I will always remember what a gift you gave me. I promise to pay it forward.

Special thanks to my friend and colleague, neighbor, and writing partner, Sarah Cedeño, who not only read the manuscript in full, but often scene by scene, fresh off the printer, as they were written. I'd stick a draft in her back door and hours later I'd have feedback. She also hashed the whole thing out with me repeatedly, patiently, while drinking wine on the porch, sitting in my living room, or over dinner at Stoneyard. Also, she was always game for helping me find new ways to commemorate my mom's death anniversary each year—frosted dragonfly cookies, sparklers in the backyard, a blue boa and champagne. I could never have done this without her.

Other friends, whether near or far, have similarly buoyed me up during the long process, listening to my frustrations and struggles, holding me together during breakdowns, cheering me on to finish. Thanks to Barb LeSavoy, Andrea Parada, Ruth Childs, Dena Levy, Sarah Freligh, Jen Litt, Silas Hansen, Rachel May, Julija Suyks, Wendy Miles, Noelle deJesus-Chua, Traci Gates, Dave Bicha, Dave DeBlieck, Birgit Kelly, Darcey Engen, and Malia Collins.

The people at Stillhouse Press have been a joy to work with and have given so much of their time and expertise to make this a great experience and a beautiful book to hold in the hands. Special thanks to Meghan McNamara, Allison Tunstall, Marcos Martinez, and Scott W. Berg for all you do. You have no idea how comforting and reassuring it is to have found myself in such good hands.

My brothers, Jim and Mike, and my sister, Amy, in particular, have been patient with me as I continued to dredge up the past and attempted to figure out what happened in our family over the years. I'm sorry for all the texts that popped up from me out of the blue, asking about difficult, painful subjects as you were simply going about your days. I know it must not have been pleasant or easy, and I thank you for answering when you could and sticking with me regardless. Amy, you have the keenest, best memory for detail and scene of anyone I know, and I want to thank you for sharing it with me as I wrote this book.

Finally, thanks to my own little family: Mark, who has seen me through the deaths of both parents and who understands, no matter what; Hudson, whose heart is kind and whose brain is on fire with ideas at all times (thanks for revamping my website, by the way); and Lily, whose wit and occasional kitchen dancing make all the stupid things in my life disappear (and way to go on picking up the trumpet out of the blue!).

And gratitude to my mother, who saved everything—I mean, everything. She was the keeper of history, the collector of memories, the stasher-away of greeting cards, paint samples, scraps of fabric, report cards, prom corsages, canceled checks, grocery lists, locks of hair, love notes. Without her beautiful, crazy archives, there's no way I could've written this book.

Anne Panning is the author of three previous fiction titles, most notably *Super America* (University of Georgia Press, 2007), which won the 2006 Flannery O'Connor Award for Short Fiction and was a *New York Times* Editor's Choice selection. Several of her nonfiction pieces have also been recognized in *The Best American Essays* series. Originally from rural Minnesota, Panning now lives in upstate New York with her husband, Mark, and two children, Hudson and Lily. She teaches creative writing at SUNY-Brockport, where she serves as Co-Director of The Brockport Writers Forum reading series, and is currently at work on her second memoir, *Bootleg Barber Shop: A Daughter's Story*, about her late father, a barber and an addict.